Second Workshop on Computational Approaches to Deception Detection (CADD 2016)

AA007978

Held at the 2016 Conference of the North American Chapter of the Association for Computational Linguistics: Human Language Technologies (NAACL HLT 2016)

San Diego, California, USA
17 June 2016

ISBN: 978-1-5108-2522-2

Printed from e-media with permission by:

Curran Associates, Inc.
57 Morehouse Lane
Red Hook, NY 12571

Some format issues inherent in the e-media version may also appear in this print version.

Copyright© (2016) by the Association for Computational Linguistics
All rights reserved.

Printed by Curran Associates, Inc. (2016)

For permission requests, please contact the Association for Computational Linguistics at the address below.

Association for Computational Linguistics
209 N. Eighth Street
Stroudsburg, Pennsylvania 18360

Phone: 1-570-476-8006
Fax: 1-570-476-0860

acl@aclweb.org

Additional copies of this publication are available from:

Curran Associates, Inc.
57 Morehouse Lane
Red Hook, NY 12571 USA
Phone: 845-758-0400
Fax: 845-758-2634
Email: curran@proceedings.com
Web: www.proceedings.com

NAACL HLT 2016

The 2016 Conference of the North American Chapter of the Association for Computational Linguistics: Human Language Technologies

Proceedings of the Second Workshop on Computational Approaches to Deception Detection CADD 2016

June 17, 2016
San Diego, California, USA

Introduction

This is the second Workshop on Computational Approaches to Deception Detection. In the first edition, held in 2012 at the European Chapter of the Association for Computational Linguistics in Avignon (France), for the first time an event was specifically dedicated to the use of computational linguistics methods for the challenges of deception detection. Indeed four years ago we collected the experience of a growing literature, which in the last 15 years began to show both the potential of NLP techniques for the evaluation of truthfulness in communication and, in parallel, possible solutions to the many challenges of the field, such as the data collection, the estimation of the ground truth, the identification of effective linguistic features and so on.

Since the beginning we were aware that the complexity of the task and the plurality of the contexts where deception can take place required a multidisciplinary approach. The present Workshop represents a step forward in that direction. We received 7 high quality submissions, accepted as papers and, in one case, for a further short tutorial. The topics range from methodological issues, to the application of NLP in a number of specific environments, such as social media, or domains that involve particular cases of deceptive information. Personal characteristics of the subjects are also considered, and their relation with linguistic and behavioral style in deceptive messages are studied. We are also pleased that methods used in typically non language-centric disciplines, such as economics, are now proposed in the field of deception detection, which suggests the possibility of new synergies between different but significant fields of research. As a total picture, we see a lively cultural environment, where new ideas arise and are brought face to face in order to facilitate and to promote the development of new solutions for the evaluation of human communication.

We would like to thank NAACL for its endorsement of the workshop. We would also like to thank the NAACL workshop co-chairs, Radu Soricut and Adrià de Gispert, and the Local Arrangements Chair, Priscilla Rasmussen, for their support. Most of all, we would like to thank our enthusiastic program committee members for their timely and thoughtful review comments. Without them, this workshop on Computational Approaches to Deception Detection could not be implemented successfully.

Organizers:

Tommaso Fornaciari, Italian National Police, Italy

Eileen Fitzpatrick. Montclair State University, Montclair NJ USA

Joan Bachenko, Linguistech LLC, Oxford NJ USA

Program Committee:

Angela Almela, University Centre for the Defense, San Javier

Iris Blandon-Gitlin, California State University, Fullerton

Claire Cardie, Cornell University

Fabio Celli, University of Trento

Rajarathnam Chandramouli, Stevens Institute of Technology

Carole Chaski, Institute for Linguistic Evidence

Walter Daelemans, University of Antwerp

Jeffrey Hancock, Stanford University

Julia Hirschberg, Columbia University

Shervin Malmasi, Harvard Medical School

Jaume Masip, University of Salamanca

Rada Mihalcea, University of Michigan

Myle Ott, Facebook

Isabel Picornell, Aston University

Massimo Poesio, University of Essex

Paolo Rosso, Universitat Politècnica de València

Victoria Rubin, University of Western Ontario

Eugene Santos, Thayer School of Engineering at Dartmouth

Carlo Strapparava, Fondazione Bruno Kessler

Lina Zhou, University of Maryland

Invited Speaker:

Rada Mihalcea, University of Michigan

Table of Contents

This page intentionally left blank.

Conference Program

Friday, June 17, 2016

9:00-10:00, keynote:

Multimodal Deception Detection using Real-life Trial Data
Rada Mihalcea

10:00-11:45, session 1

Account Deletion Prediction on RuNet: A Case Study of Suspicious Twitter Accounts Active During the Russian-Ukrainian Crisis
Svitlana Volkova and Eric Bell

Fake News or Truth? Using Satirical Cues to Detect Potentially Misleading News
Victoria Rubin, Niall Conroy, Yimin Chen and Sarah Cornwell

Using the verifiability of details as a test of deception: A conceptual framework for the automation of the verifiability approach
Bennett Kleinberg, Galit Nahari and Bruno Verschuere

11:45-12:00, Break
12:00-13:10, session 2

Estimating the Amenibility of New Domains for Deception Detection
Eileen Fitzpatrick and Joan Bachenko

The Use of Second Life for Deception Detection Research
Stephen Kunath and Kevin McCabe

13:10-15:00, Break
15:00-16:10, Session 3

Identifying Individual Differences in Gender, Ethnicity, and Personality from Dialogue for Deception Detection
Sarah Ita Levitan, Yocheved Levitan, Guozhen An, Michelle Levine, Rivka Levitan, Andrew Rosenberg and Julia Hirschberg

Individual Differences in Strategic Deception
Scott Appling and Erica Briscoe

16:10-17:00, Demo

The Use of Second Life for Deception Detection Research
Stephen Kunath and Kevin McCabe

17:00-17:30, discussion

Keynote

Multimodal Deception Detection using Real-life Trial Data

With thousands of trials and verdicts occurring daily in courtrooms around the world, the chance of using deceptive statements and testimonies as evidence is growing. In this talk, I will address the identification of deception in real-life trial data. I will present a novel dataset consisting of videos collected from public court trials, and describe a multimodal deception detection system that relies on verbal and non-verbal clues to discriminate between truthful and deceptive statements provided by defendants and witnesses. The system achieves a classification accuracy in the range of 60-75%, which exceeds by a large margin the non-expert human performance on this task. I will also describe our efforts to develop deception detection algorithms including additional modalities such as physiological sensing and thermal imaging.

This is joint work with Mihai Burzo, Mohamed Abouelenien, and Veronica Perez-Rosas.

Rada Mihalcea is a Professor in the Computer Science and Engineering department at the University of Michigan. Her research interests are in computational linguistics, with a focus on lexical semantics, multilingual natural language processing, and computational social sciences. She serves or has served on the editorial boards of the Journals of Computational Linguistics, Language Resources and Evaluations, Natural Language Engineering, Research in Language in Computation, IEEE Transactions on Affective Computing, and Transactions of the Association for Computational Linguistics. She was a program co-chair for the Conference of the Association for Computational Linguistics (2011) and the Conference on Empirical Methods in Natural Language Processing (2009), and a general chair for the Conference of the North American Chapter of the Association for Computational Linguistics (2015). She is the recipient of a National Science Foundation CAREER award (2008) and a Presidential Early Career Award for Scientists and Engineers (2009). In 2013, she was made an honorary citizen of her hometown of Cluj-Napoca, Romania.

Account Deletion Prediction on RuNet: A Case Study of Suspicious Twitter Accounts Active During the Russian-Ukrainian Crisis

Svitlana Volkova
Pacific Northwest National laboratory
902 Battelle Blvd
Richland, WA 99354
svitlana.volkova@pnnl.gov

Eric Bell
Pacific Northwest National laboratory
902 Battelle Blvd
Richland, WA 99354
Eric.Bell@pnnl.gov

Abstract

Social networks are dynamically changing over time e.g., some accounts are being created and some are being deleted or become private. This ephemerality at both an account level and content level results from a combination of privacy concerns, spam, and deceptive behaviors. In this study we analyze a large dataset of 180,340 accounts active during the Russian-Ukrainian crisis to discover a series of predictive features for the removal or shutdown of a suspicious account. We find that unlike previously reported profile and network features, lexical features form the basis for highly accurate prediction of the deletion of an account.

1 Introduction

Social media plays an important role in the life of millions of people. 1/7th of the world's population is using social media services such as Twitter, Facebook every day. There is no doubt that social media has positive effects on society by helping us to connect, communicate, access and spread information, and share our interests. Social media services have been effectively used to coordinate disaster responses (Sakaki et al., 2010), enhance emergency situational awareness (Yin et al., 2012) and coordinate crisis events (Bruno, 2011).

However, social media can potentially cause negative effects on our society. Social bots and spammers spread misinformation,[1] deceptive content, propaganda (Berger, 2015), manipulative campaigns over social networks on a large scale extremely fast e.g., several thousands retweets in a few minutes (Ferrara, 2015). Early detection of suspicious accounts that can potentially be spreading misinformation, manipulative and deceptive content is extremely important to ensure a safer and healthier environment in social media (Bamman et al., 2012b; Subrahmanian et al., 2016).

In this work we present an approach for automatically detecting deleted accounts in RuNet[2] collected during the Russian-Ukrainian crisis in 2014 - 2015. We focused on this data because news media reported several cases of misbehavior and deceptive content spread by suspended or allegedly deleted accounts on Twitter relevant to the crisis.[3] Unlike the existing work on social bot prediction (Ferrara et al., 2014), suspended account analysis (Thomas et al., 2011) and non-personal and spam user detection (Lin and Huang, 2013; Guo and Chen, 2014) we focus on a much harder task of automatically identifying fraudulent accounts (sometimes called trolls[4]). Unlike social bots or spam accounts, troll profiles on Twitter and other social networks e.g., LiveJournal, VKontakte are created to look like real users. Trolls have similar follower and friend counts as the legitimate users engage in communications with other users, express opinions etc. That's why they are very difficult to detect compared to social bots

[1] Syrian hackers claim AP hack that tipped stock market by $136 billion. Is it terrorism? (Fisher, 2013).

[2] RuNet – Russian-language community on the Internet.

[3] Inside Putin's Campaign Of Social Media Trolling And Faked Ukrainian Crimes (Gregory, 2015), Ukraine conflict: Inside Russia's 'Kremlin troll army' (Bugorkova, 2015).

[4] Europe's new cold war turns digital as Vladimir Putin expands media offensive (Boffey, 2016).

Proceedings of NAACL-HLT 2016, pages 1–6,
San Diego, California, June 12-17, 2016. ©2016 Association for Computational Linguistics

or spam accounts. Recent work on bot detection[5] analyzed 20,500 Twitter accounts that tweeted similar statements around key breaking news and events. The study suggested that bots follow many other bots, have no favorites and have no timezone, and never interact with other users through @replies and @mentions.

This is the first work that focuses on building predictive models and analyzing the effectiveness of different features to detect deleted accounts (including trolls[6]) on Twitter using deeper linguistic analysis of user-generated content in Russian and Ukrainian, sentiment and emotion features, text embeddings and topics, in addition to profile, network, and behavior clues.

2 Approach

2.1 Dataset

To collect our data we sampled Twitter accounts which used crisis-related keywords in Russian or Ukrainian[7] from the 1% Twitter feed from Mar 2014 to Mar 2015. For example, translated tweet with the crisis-relevant keywords (underlined) is: *A cache of rocket-propelled grenades was found in Kyiv which could be used for terrorist attacks.*

The original dataset had 3.5 million users who used crisis-relevant keywords during this period. We then re-crawled a random sample of 1 million accounts within a couple of months (Jun 2015) of the initial data collection (Mar 2015). We discovered that 30% of previously active accounts have been deleted. We re-crawled these accounts in Dec 2015 to validate the accounts that have been deleted as of Mar 2015 and still remain deleted as of Dec 2015. We call this portion of the data *deleted accounts* $D = 94,170$. We then randomly sampled the same number of accounts that were still active e.g., not deleted as of Mar 2015 and still remain active as of Dec 2015. We call this portion of the data *non-deleted accounts* $\bar{D} = 94,170$. For each user $u \in \{D, \bar{D}\}$ we were able to access at least 20 tweets with crisis-relevant keywords as well as user profile metadata.

2.2 Models

We used scikit-learn (Pedregosa et al., 2011) to build models that can predict deleted accounts in social media. We prefer log-linear models over reasonable alternatives e.g., perceptron or SVM, following the practice of a range of previous work in related areas (Smith, 2004; Liu et al., 2005; Poon et al., 2009; Bamman et al., 2012a; Filippova, 2012; Volkova and Bachrach, 2015; Hovy, 2015).

In Table 1 we outline a comprehensive list of features we used to our build models. We significantly expanded the list of features that have been previously used for bot detection on Twitter (Ferrara et al., 2014). In addition to previously used account and behavior features our models rely on deeper linguistic analysis of content (tweets) generated by users, topics and embeddings, as well as visual and affect (sentiment and emotion) features. We outline the details on how we extracted lexical and affect features below.

BoW features Since Russian and Ukrainian are morphologically rich languages, to reduce sparsity and ensure better model generalization, we lemmatized words using pymorphy2 package.[8] We extracted bag-of-word (BoW) features from preprocessed lemmatized tweets; we also excluded all stopwords and words with frequency less than five; we run our experiments varying word ngram size (unigrams, bigrams and trigrams) for binary vs. normalized frequency-based features.

LSA features We performed linear dimensionality reduction on feature vectors extracted using BoW normalized frequency-based features as described above using Latent Semantic Analysis (Dumais, 2004) implemented as truncated Singular Value Decomposition (SVD) in scikit-learn.[9] Similarly, we

[5] Social Network Analysis Reveals Full Scale of Kremlin's Twitter Bot Campaign (Lawrence, 2015).

[6] We can not guarantee that these accounts might be potentially spreading deceptive content. However, after manual inspection of the tweets from 100 deleted accounts we found that all 100 accounts display characteristics and behavior shared by those involved in spreading deceptive content, for example, they only post/repost tweets relevant to crisis, there is high ngram/string similarity among their tweets.

[7] Our lexicon of crisis-related keywords has been built independently by three native speakers of Russian and Ukrainian. The final lexicon contains 53 keywords in both languages e.g., Crimea, revolution, Donetsk, ceasefire, NATO, EU etc.

[8] https://pypi.python.org/pypi/pymorphy2

[9] http://scikit-learn.org/stable/modules/generated/sklearn.decomposition.TruncatedSVD.html

performed linear dimensionality reduction on feature vectors extracted using hashtags and mentions. We varied the number of dimensions $c = [50, 100, 500]$ to get the best F1 and report the results for $c = 100$.

LDA features We learned topics using Latent Dirichlet Allocation (LDA)[10] (Blei et al., 2003) on 1 million tweets randomly sampled from the original 3.5 million tweets. We varied the number of topics $t = [50, 100, 250, 500, 1000]$, and optimized α and β priors by minimizing log-likelihood. We report the results for $t = 1000$, $\alpha = 0.1$ and $\beta = 0.005$.

Embeddings We learned word embeddings for Russian using Word2Vec's skip-gram and CBOW models (Mikolov et al., 2013) implemented in gensim package[11] with a layer size of 50. The embeddings are learned on the same corpus of 1 million tweets as LDA topics. After learning embeddings, we assign words to clusters by measuring cosine similarity between two word embeddings, and compute clusters using spectral clustering over a word-word similarity matrix.

Affect features Finally, to extract sentiment features we predict polarity score for every tweet for each user using the state-of-the-art sentiment classification system for Russian developed by Chetviorkin et al. (2014), Loukachevitch and Chetviorkin (2014). Polarity scores vary around 0 (neutral) between -2 (negative) and +2 (positive). We calculate mean polarity scores, and the proportions of positive, negative and neutral tweets for every user (Dickerson et al., 2014).

To extract emotion features, we predict one of six Ekman's emotions such as: sadness, joy, fear, disgust, surprise and anger for each tweet using an approach recently developed by Mohammad and Kiritchenko (2015) and Volkova and Bachrach (2015). Similar to sentiment features, we use six emotion proportions per user as features.

Profile (account and behavior) features $\vert f^{prof}\vert = 12$
days since account creation, number of followers, number of friends, number of favorites, number of tweets, friend-to-follow ratio, name length in chars, bio in chars, screen name length in chars, screen name length in words, bio length words, avg. number of tweets per hour
Visual features $\vert f^{vis}\vert = 658$
bag-of-words (BoW) on profile background color, profile link color, text color, sidebar color, background tile, sidebar border color, default profile image
Syntactic features $\vert f^{syn}\vert = 14$
aver. tweet length in words, aver. tweet length in chars, retweet rate: prop. of RTs to tweets, uppercase word rate, elongated word rate, repeated mixed punctuation rate, prop. of tweets with links, tweets that are retweets (RTs), prop. of tweets with mentions, hashtags, punctuation, emoticons, mention, hashtag, url rate per word
Network features $\vert f^{men}\vert = 159,563$, $\vert f^{ht}\vert = 7,983$
mentioned and retweeted users (@mentions), LSA on @mentions with $c = [50, 100, 500]$ dimensions, BoW on hashtags, LSA on hashtags with $c = [50, 100, 500]$
Lexical features $\vert f^{lex}\vert = 110,302$
bag-of-words (BoW) on tweets, LSA on tweets, LDA on tweets with $t = [50, 100, 250, 500, 1000]$ topics embeddings with $d = [30, 50, \ldots, 2000]$ dimensions
Affect (sentiment and emotion) features $\vert f^{affect}\vert = 12$
number of emoticons, prop. of emotions, mean scores, prop. of tweets with positive, negative, neutral sentiment,

Table 1: Profile, visual, lexical, network and affect features used for account deletion prediction.

3 Experimental Results

3.1 Classification Results

In Table 3 we present account deletion classification results using individual feature types. We report our results using 10-fold cross validation on a balanced set of 188,340 deleted and non-deleted accounts.

We found that lexical features are the most predictive yielding F1 as high as 0.87. Interestingly, we found that frequency-based features outperform binary features. *It means that for account deletion prediction it is not only important what the users say but how much they say it.* We also found that higher order ngrams only slightly outperform unigram features. When the dimensionality of the feature space is reduced from 110K to 1000 (Embeddings), 1,000 (LDA), and 100 (LSA), classification results drop by 0.11, 0.06 and 0.03, respectively. Syntactic features extracted using shallow linguistic analysis demonstrate lower F1 than lexical features, but higher F1 of 0.81 than the rest of non-lexical features.

Similar to earlier work, we found that profile features have high predictive power for detecting deleted accounts yielding F1 as high as 0.85. Network features have moderate predictive power,

[10] https://pypi.python.org/pypi/lda

[11] https://radimrehurek.com/gensim/models/word2vec.html

Feature Type	Example features sorted by predictive power for deleted D and non-deleted $\bar{D}$ accounts
Lexical	D: end, cressid, sokrin, alphabet, web money, haim, master, video segment, klyati, forest restoration $\bar{D}$: arbi, mes, venta, lambesis, cozy, nikolay, restrict, agreement, perl, chubais, ethernet, insulation
Hashtags	D: #volkswagen, #win, #meat, #slovenia, #therewillneverbeanotheronedirection, #crishtian, #kebab $\bar{D}$: #brent, #novorussia, #gromaidan, #leg, #hydroelectric, #media, #plantyourowntree, #underwater
Mentions	D: @newskazru, @volumesocial, @whafar, @max_7korolei, @chernyj1974, @dreamknoxville $\bar{D}$: @agnfkvvaalena, blascepna72, @chico6, @xagiqasez, @kathrynbruscobk, @deanarianda
Topics	D: 337: beat up, resolve, press office, parliamentarian, intimidation; 376: accountability, position $\bar{D}$: 792: reach, captain, fluffy, quit the job, shoot, satellite; 310: quarter, hitchcock, pitting, ensue

Table 2: The most discriminative unigrams, hashtags, mentions and topics (translated) for account deletion prediction.

Feature Type	F1	P	R
Profile			
Account + behavior	**0.85**	0.84	0.86
Visual	**0.73**	0.65	0.83
Language			
Syntactic	0.81	0.77	0.85
BoW tweets	**0.87**	**0.89**	**0.86**
LSA tweets	0.84	0.89	0.79
LDA tweets	0.81	0.85	0.78
Embeddings	0.76	0.68	0.85
Network			
Hashtags	0.76	0.63	0.96
LSA hashtags	0.73	0.59	0.97
Mentions	**0.78**	0.66	0.96
LSA mentions	0.72	0.60	0.91
Affect			
Sentiment + emotion	**0.72**	0.64	0.81
ALL	**0.82**	**0.79**	**0.88**

Table 3: Classification results in terms of F1, precision (P), and recall (R) based on individual feature types.

with mentions demonstrating F1=0.78 and hashtags F1=0.76. Interestingly, unlike lexical features, binary and frequency-based mention and hashtag features demonstrate equal classification results. *It means that for account deletion prediction it is not important how much the users use some hashtags or @mentions, but whether they use them or not.* Finally, sentiment and emotion features yield comparable F1 of 0.72 to visual features.

3.2 Feature Analysis

To show that the differences between deleted and non-deleted accounts are statistically significant we performed a Mann-Whitney U-test on account, affect and syntactic features (Mann and Whitney, 1947). We found all differences to be significant (p-value ≤ 0.001). We outline our key findings below.

Profile differences Deleted accounts have less followers than non-deleted accounts, but they have more friends. They have less favorites than non-deleted, as well as the tweets, and significantly lower friend-to-follower ratio. Deleted account have significantly shorter bios, but longer user names.

Syntactic differences Deleted accounts generate shorter tweets, use less elongated words, capitalized words and repeated punctuation. They have lower hashtag, mention and url per word ratios. They produce significantly less retweets, tweets with hashtags, urls and mentions, tweets with punctuations and emoticons than non-deleted accounts.

Sentiment and emotion differences Deleted accounts produce *less positive tweets, more negative and more neutral tweets* compared to non-deleted accounts. Deleted accounts *express less anger, but significantly more sadness and fear in their tweets.* Both account types produce comparable amounts of joy, disgust and surprise emotions.

We present the examples of the most discriminative ngram, mention, hashtag and topic features learned by our models in Table 2.

4 Conclusion

We presented the first work on suspicious account deletion prediction in RuNet. We analyzed the predictive power of a variety of previously unexplored features including lexical, topics, hashtags, mentions, sentiments and emotions, in addition to the existing profile and behavior features. We found that deleted and non-deleted accounts on Twitter not only have different profiles, but also express significant differences in topics, hashtags and lexical terms they mention, the ways they generate tweets (syntactic differences), as well as sentiments and emotions they express. All of these differences allow building highly accurate models for detecting suspicious accounts in social media.

References

David Bamman, Jacob Eisenstein, and Tyler Schnoebelen. 2012a. Gender in twitter: Styles, stances, and social networks. *CoRR abs/1210.4567*.

David Bamman, Brendan O'Connor, and Noah Smith. 2012b. Censorship and deletion practices in chinese social media. *First Monday*, 17(3).

J.M. Berger. 2015. The evolution of terrorist propaganda: The paris attack and social media. http://www.brookings.edu/research/testimony/2015/01/27-terrorist-propaganda-/social-media-berger.

David M Blei, Andrew Y Ng, and Michael I Jordan. 2003. Latent dirichlet allocation. *Journal of Machine Learning Research*, 3:993–1022.

Daniel Boffey. 2016. Europe's new cold war turns digital as vladimir putin expands media offensive. http://www.theguardian.com/world/2016/mar/05/europe-vladimir-putin-russia-/social-media-trolls.

Nicola Bruno. 2011. Tweet first, verify later? How real-time information is changing the coverage of worldwide crisis events. *Oxford: Reuters Institute for the Study of Journalism, University of Oxford. Retrieved June*, 10(2011):2010–2011.

Olga Bugorkova. 2015. Ukraine conflict: Inside russia's 'Kremlin troll army'. http://www.bbc.com/news/world-europe-31962644.

Ilia Chetviorkin, Leninskiye Gory Moscow, and Natalia Loukachevitch. 2014. Two-step model for sentiment lexicon extraction from Twitter streams. *Proceedings of ACL*, pages 67–72.

John P Dickerson, Vadim Kagan, and VS Subrahmanian. 2014. Using sentiment to detect bots on Twitter: Are humans more opinionated than bots? In *Proceedings of ASONAM*, pages 620–627.

Susan T Dumais. 2004. Latent semantic analysis. *Annual review of information science and technology*, 38(1):188–230.

Emilio Ferrara, Onur Varol, Clayton Davis, Filippo Menczer, and Alessandro Flammini. 2014. The rise of social bots. *arXiv preprint arXiv:1407.5225*.

Emilio Ferrara. 2015. Manipulation and abuse on social media. *arXiv preprint arXiv:1503.03752*.

Katja Filippova. 2012. User demographics and language in an implicit social network. In *Proceedings of EMNLP-CoNLL*, pages 1478–1488.

Max Fisher. 2013. Syrian hackers claim ap hack that tipped stock market by $136 billion. Is it terrorism? https://www.washingtonpost.com/news/worldviews/wp/2013/04/23/syrian-hackers-claim-ap-hack-that-tipped-stock-market-by-136-billion-is-it-terrorism/.

Paul Roderick Gregory. 2015. Inside putin's campaign of social media trolling and faked ukrainian crimes. http://www.forbes.com/sites/paulroderickgregory/2014/05/11/inside-putins-campaign-of-social/-media-trolling-and-faked-ukrainian/-crimes/#97c1e9629db0.

Diansheng Guo and Chao Chen. 2014. Detecting non-personal and spam users on geo-tagged Twitter network. *Transactions in GIS*, 18(3):370–384.

Dirk Hovy. 2015. Demographic factors improve classification performance. *Proceedings of ACL*, pages 752–762.

Alexander Lawrence. 2015. Social network analysis reveals full scale of Kremlin's Twitter bot campaign. https://globalvoices.org/2015/04/02/analyzing-kremlin-twitter-bots/.

Po-Ching Lin and Po-Min Huang. 2013. A study of effective features for detecting long-surviving twitter spam accounts. In *Proceedings of ICACT*, pages 841–846.

Yang Liu, Qun Liu, and Shouxun Lin. 2005. Log-linear models for word alignment. In *Proceedings of the Annual Meeting on Association for Computational Linguistics (ACL)*, pages 459–466.

Natalia Loukachevitch and Ilia Chetviorkin. 2014. Open evaluation of sentiment-analysis systems based on the material of the russian language. *Scientific and Technical Information Processing*, 41(6):370–376.

Henry B Mann and Donald R Whitney. 1947. On a test of whether one of two random variables is stochastically larger than the other. *The Annals of Mathematical Statistics*, pages 50–60.

Tomas Mikolov, Kai Chen, Greg Corrado, and Jeffrey Dean. 2013. Efficient estimation of word representations in vector space. *arXiv preprint arXiv:1301.3781*.

Saif M Mohammad and Svetlana Kiritchenko. 2015. Using hashtags to capture fine emotion categories from tweets. *Computational Intelligence*, 31(2):301–326.

Fabian Pedregosa, Gal Varoquaux, Alexandre Gramfort, Vincent Michel, Bertrand Thirion, Olivier Grisel, Mathieu Blondel, Peter Prettenhofer, Ron Weiss, Vincent Dubourg, Jake Vanderplas, Alexandre Passos, David Cournapeau, Matthieu Brucher, Matthieu Perrot, and Douard Duchesnay. 2011. Scikit-learn: Machine Learning in Python. *Journal of Machine Learning Research*, 12:2825–2830.

Hoifung Poon, Colin Cherry, and Kristina Toutanova. 2009. Unsupervised morphological segmentation with log-linear models. In *Proceedings of NAACL*, pages 209–217.

Takeshi Sakaki, Makoto Okazaki, and Yutaka Matsuo. 2010. Earthquake shakes twitter users: real-time event detection by social sensors. In *Proceedings of WWW*, pages 851–860. ACM.

Noah A. Smith. 2004. Log-linear models.

VS Subrahmanian, Amos Azaria, Skylar Durst, Vadim Kagan, Aram Galstyan, Kristina Lerman, Linhong

Zhu, Emilio Ferrara, Alessandro Flammini, Filippo Menczer, et al. 2016. The DARPA Twitter Bot Challenge. *arXiv preprint arXiv:1601.05140*.

Kurt Thomas, Chris Grier, Dawn Song, and Vern Paxson. 2011. Suspended accounts in retrospect: an analysis of twitter spam. In *Proceedings of the ACM SIGCOMM Conference on Internet Measurement Conference*, pages 243–258. ACM.

Svitlana Volkova and Yoram Bachrach. 2015. On predicting sociodemographic traits and emotions from communications in social networks and their implications to online self-disclosure. *Cyberpsychology, Behavior, and Social Networking*, 18(12):726–736.

Jie Yin, Andrew Lampert, Mark Cameron, Bella Robinson, and Robert Power. 2012. Using social media to enhance emergency situation awareness. *IEEE Intelligent Systems*, (6):52–59.

Fake News or Truth?
Using Satirical Cues to Detect Potentially Misleading News.

Victoria L. Rubin, Niall J. Conroy, Yimin Chen, and Sarah Cornwell
Language and Information Technology Research Lab (LIT.RL)
Faculty of Information and Media Studies
University of Western Ontario, London, Ontario, CANADA
vrubin@uwo.ca, nconroy1@uwo.ca, ychen582@uwo.ca, scornwel@uwo.ca

Abstract

Satire is an attractive subject in deception detection research: it is a type of deception that intentionally incorporates cues revealing its own deceptiveness. Whereas other types of fabrications aim to instill a false sense of truth in the reader, a successful satirical hoax must eventually be exposed as a jest. This paper provides a conceptual overview of satire and humor, elaborating and illustrating the unique features of satirical news, which mimics the format and style of journalistic reporting. Satirical news stories were carefully matched and examined in contrast with their legitimate news counterparts in 12 contemporary news topics in 4 domains (civics, science, business, and "soft" news). Building on previous work in satire detection, we proposed an SVM-based algorithm, enriched with 5 predictive features (*Absurdity, Humor, Grammar, Negative Affect,* and *Punctuation*) and tested their combinations on 360 news articles. Our best predicting feature combination (*Absurdity, Grammar* and *Punctuation*) detects satirical news with a 90% precision and 84% recall (F-score=87%). Our work in algorithmically identifying satirical news pieces can aid in minimizing the potential deceptive impact of satire.

1. Introduction

In the course of news production, dissemination, and consumption, there are ample opportunities to deceive and be deceived. Direct falsifications such as journalistic fraud or social media hoaxes pose obvious predicaments. While fake or satirical news may be less malicious, they may still mislead inattentive readers. Taken at face value, satirical news can intentionally create a false belief in the readers' minds, per classical definitions of deception (Buller & Burgoon, 1996; Zhou, Burgoon, Nunamaker, & Twitchell, 2004). The falsehoods are intentionally poorly concealed, and beg to be unveiled. Yet some readers simply miss the joke, and the fake news is further propagated, with often costly consequences (Rubin, Chen, & Conroy, 2015).

1.1. The News Context

In recent years, there has been a trend towards decreasing confidence in the mainstream media. According to Gallup polls, only 40% of Americans trust their mass media sources to report the news "fully, accurately and fairly" (Riffkin, 2015) and a similar survey in the UK has shown that the most-read newspapers were also the least-trusted (Reilly & Nye, 2012). One effect of this trend has been to drive news readers to rely more heavily on alternative information sources, including blogs and social media, as a means to escape the perceived bias and unreliability of mainstream news (Tsfati, 2010). Ironically, this may leave the readers even more susceptible to incomplete, false, or misleading information (Mocanu, Rossi, Zhang, Karsai, & Quattrociocchi, 2015).

In general, humans are fairly ineffective at recognizing deception (DePaulo, Charlton, Cooper, Lindsay, & Muhlenbruck, 1997; Rubin & Conroy, 2012; Vrij, Mann, & Leal, 2012). A number of factors may explain why. First, most people show an inherent truth-bias (Van Swol, 2014): they tend to assume that the information they receive is true and reliable. Second, some people seem to exhibit a "general gullibility" (Pennycook, Cheyne, Barr, Koehler, & Fugelsang, 2015) and are inordinately receptive to ideas that they do not fully understand. Third, confirmation bias can cause people to simply see only what they want to see – conservative

Proceedings of NAACL-HLT 2016, pages 7–17,
San Diego, California, June 12-17, 2016. ©2016 Association for Computational Linguistics

viewers of the news satire program *the Colbert Report*, for example, tend to believe that the comedian's statements are sincere, while liberal viewers tend to recognize the satirical elements (LaMarre, Landreville, & Beam, 2009).

1.2. Problem Statement

High rates of media consumption and low trust in news institutions create an optimal environment for the "rapid viral spread of information that is either intentionally or unintentionally misleading or provocative" (Howell, 2013). Journalists and other content producers are incentivized towards speed and spectacle over accuracy (Chen, Conroy, & Rubin, 2015) and content consumers often lack the literacy skills required to interpret news critically (Hango, 2014). What is needed for both content producers and consumers is an automated assistive tool that can save time and cognitive effort by flagging/filtering inaccurate or false information.

In developing such a tool, we have chosen news satire as a starting point for the investigation of deliberate deception in news. Unlike subtler forms of deception, satire may feature more obvious cues that reveal its disassociation from truth because the objective of satire is for at least some subset of readers to recognize the joke (Pfaff & Gibbs, 1997). And yet, articles from *The Onion* and other satirical news sources are often shared and even reprinted in newspapers as if the stories were true[1]. In other words, satirical news may mislead readers who are unaware of the satirical nature of news, or lacking in the contextual or cultural background to interpret the fake as such. In this paper, we examine the textual features of satire and test for the most reliable cues in differentiating satirical news from legitimate news.

2. Literature Review

2.1. Satire

As a concept, satire has been remarkably hard to pin down in the scholarly literature (Condren, 2012). One framework for humor, proposed by Ziv (1988), suggests five discrete categories of humor: aggressive, sexual, social, defensive, and intellectual. Satire, according to Simpson (2003), is complicated because it occupies more than one place in the framework: it clearly has an aggressive and social function, and often expresses an intellectual aspect as well. From this, satire can be conceptualized as "a rhetorical strategy (in any medium) that seeks wittily to provoke an emotional and intellectual reaction in an audience on a matter of public ... significance" (Phiddian, 2013).

On the attack, satirical works use a variety of rhetorical devices, such as hyperbole, absurdity, and obscenity, in order to shock or unease readers. Traditionally, satire has been divided into two main styles: Juvenalian, the more overtly hostile of the two, and Horatian, the more playful (Condren, 2014). Juvenalian satire is characterized by contempt and sarcasm and an often aggressively pessimistic worldview (e.g., Swift's *A Modest Proposal*). Horatian satire, by contrast, tends more towards teasing, mockery, and black humor (e.g., Kubrick's *Dr. Strangelove*). In each, there is a mix of both laughter and scorn – though Juvenalian tends towards scorn, some hint of laughter must be present and vice versa for Horatian.

Satire must also serve a purpose beyond simple spectacle: it must aspire "to cure folly and to punish evil" (Highet, 1972: 156). It is not enough to simply mock a target; some form of critique or call to action is required. This "element of censoriousness" or "ethically critical edge" (Condren, 2012: 378) supplies the social commentary that separates satire from mere invective. However, the receptiveness of an audience to satire's message depends upon a level of "common agreement" (Frye, 1944: 76) between the writer and the reader that the target is worthy of both disapproval and ridicule. This is one way that satire may miss its mark with some readers: they might recognize the satirist's critique, but simply disagree with his or her position.

As a further confounding factor, satire does not speak its message plainly, and hides its critique in irony and double-meanings. Though satire aims to attack the folly and evil of others, it also serves to highlight the intelligence and wit of its author. Satire makes use of opposing scripts, text that is compatible with two different readings (Simpson, 2003: 30), to achieve this effect. The incongruity between the two scripts is part of what makes satire funny (e.g., when Stephen Colbert, states "I give people the truth, unfiltered by rational argu-

1 See: https://www.washingtonpost.com/news/worldviews/wp/2015/06/02/7-times-the-onion-was-lost-in-translation

ment."[2]), but readers who fail to grasp the humor become, themselves, part of the joke. In this way, we consider satire a type of deception, but one that is intended to be found out by at least some subset of the audience. Although "the author mostly assumes that readers will recover the absurdity of the created text, which hopefully will prompt the readers to consider issues beyond the text" (Pfaff & Gibbs, 1997), what one reader considers absurd might be perfectly reasonable to another.

In his *Anatomy of Satire*, Highet distinguishes satire from other forms of "lies and exaggerations intended to deceive" (1972: 92). Whereas other types of fabrications and swindles aim to instill a false sense of truth in the reader, which benefits the deceiver for as long as it remains undiscovered, a successful satirical hoax must eventually be exposed. After all, an author of satire cannot be appreciated for his or her wit if no one recognizes the joke. This interpretation of satire is in line with Hopper & Bell's (1984) category of "benign fabrications," which include make believe, jokes, and teasing – types of deception that are generally both socially acceptable and fairly easy to uncover.

2.2. Satire in News

News satire is a genre of satire that mimics the format and style of journalistic reporting. The fake news stories are typically inspired by real ones, and cover the same range of subject matter: from politics to weather to crime. The satirical aspect arises when the factual basis of the story is "comically extended to a fictitious construction where it becomes incongruous or even absurd, in a way that intersects entertainment with criticism" (Ermida, 2012: 187). News satire is most often presented in the Horatian style, where humor softens the impact of harshness of the critique – the spoonful of sugar that helps the medicine go down. More than mere lampoon, fake news stories aim to "arouse the readers' attention, amuse them, and at the same time awaken their capacity to judge contemporary society" (Ermida, 2012: 188).

With the rise of the internet, news satire sites such as *The Onion* have become a prolific part of the media ecosystem. Stories from satirical sources are frequently shared over social media, where they deceive at least some of their readers. Indeed, people are fooled often enough that internet sites such as Literally Unbelievable (Hongo, 2016) have sprung up to document these instances.

Several factors contribute to the believability of fake news online. Recent polls have found that only 60% of Americans read beyond the headline (The Media Insight Project, 2014). Furthermore, on social media platforms like Facebook and Twitter, stories which are "liked" or "shared" all appear in a common visual format. Unless a user looks specifically for the source attribution, an article from *The Onion* looks just like an article from a credible source, like *The New York Times*. In an effort to counteract this trend, we propose the creation of an automatic satire detection system.

So, how can satirical news stories be identified? Ermida (2012: 194-195) proposes the model of parodic news satire in Figure 1.

COMPONENTS OF PARODIC NEWS SATIRE

I	II	III
INTERTEXTUAL COMPONENT	CRITICAL COMPONENT	COMIC COMPONENT
I.a) Structural component		III.a) Lexical component
I.b) Stylistic component		III.b) Pragmatic component
		III.c) Rhetorical component

Figure 1: Ermida's (2012) model of satirical news.

For the purposes of this research, we focus on component III to inform our investigation into cues to differentiate news satire from legitimate news reporting. The next section overviews satirical news detection efforts to date and positions them as beneficial in the deception detection research.

3. Detection Methodology Review

The methods described in this review demonstrate promising results for satire and humor detection. The goal of screening legitimate news content is achieved based on the assumption that successful identification of satire is independent from both the originating source of the piece, and its provenance as a news document. Instead, Natural Language Processing (NLP) methods in combination with machine learning deal with content directly by detecting language patterns, topicality, sentiment, rhetorical devices and word occurrences which are common to satire and irony. There is a need for a unified approach that combines best practices for a comprehensive NLP satire detection system.

2 2006 White House Correspondents Dinner: https://youtu.be/2X93u3anTco

3.1. Word Level Features

Burfoot & Baldwin (2009) attempted to determine whether or not newswire articles can be automatically classified as satirical. The approach relied on lexical and semantic features such as headlines, profanity, or slang, as well as support vector machines (SVMs) on simple bag-of-words features which were supplemented with feature weighting. Similar attempts have used corpus-based relatedness which uses cosine similarity and tf*idf weighting. At the granularity of individual words and *n*-grams, text cues can point to the presence of satire, for example counterfactual words ("nevertheless", "yet"), and temporal compression words ("now", "abruptly") (Mihalcea, Strapparava, & Pulman, 2010). As a base measure, tf*idf on bigrams provided F-score of roughly 65%. The use of additional features derived from semantic analysis heuristics improved classifier performance on joke detection. Using combined joke specific features led to 84% precision, demonstrating synergistic effect of feature combination.

We hypothesize expanding the possibilities of word-level analysis by measuring the utility of features like part of speech frequency, and semantic categories such as generalizing terms, time/space references, positive and negative polarity. In addition, we incorporate the use of exaggerated language (e.g., profanity, slang, grammar markers) and frequent run-on sentences. We take these features as indicators of satirical rhetoric component (III.c, per Ermida, 2012).

3.2. Semantic Validity

Satirical news contains a higher likelihood of imbalances between concepts expressing temporal consistency, as well as contextual imbalances (Reyes, Rosso, & Buscaldi, 2012), for example, well known people in unexpected settings. A similar idea of unexpectedness was explored by Burfoot and Baldwin (2009) who measured the presence of absurdity by defining a notion of "semantic validity": true news stories found on the web will contain differences in the presence of co-occurring named entities than those entities found in satire. Shallow and deep linguistic layers may represent relevant information to identify figurative uses of language. For example, ontological semantics such as ambiguity and incongruity, and meta-linguistic devices, such as polarity and emotional scenarios can achieve precision accuracy of 80% for classifying humorous tweets (Reyes et al., 2012). Semantically disparate concepts can also influence absurdity, when judged based on semantic relatedness (distance in WordNet hierarchy), summed and normalized (Reyes & Rosso, 2014). In this study, we use this measure of absurdity as an indicator of the pragmatic component (II.b) of satirical news (Ermida, 2012).

3.3. Humor and Opposing Scripts

Sjöbergh and Araki (2007) presented a machine learning approach for classifying sentences as one-liner jokes or normal sentences. Instead of deep analysis, they rely on weighting derived from a combination of simple features like word overlap with a joke corpus, and ambiguity (number of *dictionary.com* word senses), achieving an 85% accuracy. The incongruity (resolution) theory is a theory of comprehension which depends on the introduction of "latent terms". Humor is found when two scripts overlap and oppose. As a joke narration evolves, some "latent" terms are gradually introduced, which set the joke on a train of thought. Yet because of ambiguous quality of the terms, the humorous input advances on two or more interpretation paths. The interpretation shifts suddenly from the starting point of the initial sequence:

> *"Is the doctor at home?" the patient asked in a whisper. "No", the doctor's pretty wife whispered back, "Come right in."* (Attardo, Hempelmann, & Mano, 2002: 35)

The latter path gains more importance as elements are added to the current interpretation of the reader, and eventually ends up forming the punch line of the joke (Hempelmann, Raskin, & Triezenberg, 2006). To detect opposing scripts, Polanyi and Zaenen (2006) suggest a theoretical framework in which the context of sentiment words shifts the valence of the expressed sentiment. Hempelmann et al. (2006) employed Text Meaning Representations (TMRs) which are data models aimed at preserving vagueness in language while using an ontology representation from a fact repository, a pre-processor, and an analyzer to transform text. They propose an identification method by checking the number of word senses of the last word that "make sense" in the current context, although no performance evaluation is provided.

Other means of joke classification rely on naive Bayes and SVM based on joke-specific features, including polysemy and Latent Semantic Analysis (LSA) trained on joke data, as well as semantic relatedness. Mihalcea and Liu (2006) and Mihalcea and Pulman (2007) presented such a system that relies on metrics including knowledge-based similarity (path between concepts) and corpus based similarity (term co-occurrence from large corpus). They conclude that the most frequently observed semantic features are negative polarity and human-centeredness. A correct punch line, which generates surprise, has a minimum relatedness with respect to the set-up. The highest overall precision of 84% was obtained with models that rely on joke-specific features, with the LSA model trained on a jokes corpus (Mihalcea et al., 2010). These methods informed our investigation of Ermida's lexical component (III.a) (2012).

Past research in humor detection provides useful heuristics for NLP. A shortcoming is that best practices have yet to be combined in a comprehensive detection methodology. For example, punchline detection may be employed to longer, discourse layer content beyond mere one liners, through the comparison of constituent text segments. Absurdity, measured through the presence of atypical named entities, may be extended to other contexts. Our examination of satire sources hints at the tendency to introduce new, unfamiliar named entities at the end of news articles as a form of ironic non-sequitur.

3.4. Recognizing Sarcasm and Irony

Recognition of sarcasm can benefit many sentiment analysis applications and the identification of fake news. Sarcasm is defined as "verbal irony … the activity of saying or writing the opposite of what you mean" (Tsur, Davidov, & Rappoport, 2010). Utsumi (2000) introduced a cognitive computational framework that models the ironic environment from an axiomatic system depending heavily on "world knowledge" and expectations. It requires analysis of each utterance and its context to match predicates in a specific logical formalism. Davidov, Tsur, and Rappoport (2010) looked for elements to automatically detect sarcasm in online products reviews, achieving a 77% precision and 83% recall. They proposed surface features (information about the product, company, title, etc.), frequent words or punctuation marks, to represent sarcastic texts. Ironic expressions often use such markers to safely realize their communicative effects (e.g., '*'Trees died for this book?"* - book review; *"All the features you want. Too bad they don't work!"* - smart phone review). Beyond grammar and word polarity, emotional scenarios capture irony in terms of elements which symbolize abstractions such as overall sentiments and moods. Presence of humor may be correlated to polarity of positive/negative semantic orientation and emotiveness. Using Twitter content, models of irony detection were assessed along these linguistic characteristics, and positive results provide valuable insights into figurative speech in the task of sentiment analysis (Reyes & Rosso, 2014; Reyes, Rosso, & Veale, 2013).

4. Methodology

4.1. Dataset and Data Collection Methods

In this study we collected and analyzed a dataset of 360 news articles as a wide-ranging and diverse data sample, representative of the scope of US and Canadian national newspapers. The dataset was collected in 2 sets. The first set was collected from 2 satirical news sites (*The Onion* and *The Beaverton*) and 2 legitimate news sources (*The Toronto Star* and *The New York Times*) in 2015. The 240 articles were aggregated by a 2 x 2 x 4 x 3 design (US/Canadian; satirical/legitimate online news; varying across 4 domains (civics, science, business, and "soft" news) with 3 distinct topics within each of the 4 domains (see Table 1).

CIVICS	SCIENCE	BUSINESS	"SOFT" NEWS
Gun Violence	Environment	Tech	Celebrity
Immigration	Health	Finance	Sports
Elections	Other Sciences	Corporate Announcements	Local News

Table 1: Sample News Topicality. 5 Canadian and 5 American satirical and legitimate article pairs were collected on 12 topics across 4 domains.

For each of the 12 topics, 5 Canadian (from *The Beaverton*) and 5 American (from *the Onion*) satirical articles were collected. Each satirical piece was then matched to a legitimate news article that was published in the same country, and as closely related in subject matter as possible. For example, in the Environment topic, the *Beaverton* article "Invasive homo sapiens species meet at forestry conference to discuss pine beetles" was paired with a *Toronto Star* article on invasive species: "'Dangerous and invasive' Khapra beetle intercepted at Pearson". See Figure 2 for the pairing of the articles about Hillary Clinton in the Elections topic.

Figure 2: Two news articles about Hillary Clinton: from the Onion and The New York Times.

An additional set of 120 articles was collected in 2016 to expand the inventory of sources and topics, and to serve as a reliability test for the manual findings within the first set. The second set, still evenly distributed between satirical and legitimate news, was drawn from 6 legitimate[3] and 6 satirical[4] North American online news sources.

Analysis: A trained linguist content-analyzed each pair (legitimate vs. satirical), looking for insights on similarities and differences as well as trends in language use and rhetorical devices. For machine learning we used the combined set of 360, reserving random 25% of the combined 2 sets data for testing, and performing 10-fold cross-validation on the training set. The complete dataset is available from the lab's public website[5].

5. Results

5.1. Data-Driven Linguistic Observations

Absurdity and Humor: Similar to Burfoot & Baldwin (2009), we found that the headlines were especially relevant to detecting satire. While legitimate news articles report new material in the first line, satirical articles tend to repeat material from the title. We also found the final line of each article relevant to satire detection. In particular, the final line was commonly a "punchline" that highlighted absurdities in the story or introduced a new element to the joke. This humorous function diverges sharply from the standard "inverted pyramid" article structure of legitimate news articles, and it proved useful in identifying satirical journalism.

These observations informed the selection of 2 features: *Absurdity* and *Humor*. For example, the final line of *The Beaverton*'s "Scientists at University of the Lord discover that Jesus is Lord" introduces new named entities (indicating absurdity) and is semantically dissimilar (indicating humor) from the remainder of the article:

> *"At press time, researchers from Christopher Hitchens Memorial University discovered that it was fun to drink a lot of Johnny Walker Red Label and call people sheep."*

We also observed a high frequency of slang and swear words in the satirical news pieces, but unlike Burfoot and Baldwin (2009), for our dataset these features did not add predictive powers.

Sentence Complexity: A noticeable syntactic difference between the satirical and legitimate articles was sentence length and complexity. Especially for quotations, the satirical articles tend to pack a greater number of clauses into a sentence for comedic effect. For example, compare these two excerpts - the first from *The Onion*, and the second from its paired article in *The New York Times*:

> *(1) "Not too long ago, these early people were alive and going about their normal daily lives, but sadly, by the time we scaled down the narrow 90-meter chute leading into the cave, they'd already been dead for at least 10,000 decades," said visibly upset University of the Witwatersrand paleoanthropologist Lee R. Berger, bemoaning the fact that they could have saved the group of human predecessors if they had just reached the Rising Star cave system during the Pleistocene epoch." - The Onion* "Tearful Anthropologists Discover Dead Ancestor of Humans 100,000 Years Too Late".

> *(2) "With almost every bone in the body represented multiple times, Homo naledi is already practically the best-known fossil member of our lineage," Dr. Berger said." - The New York Times* "Homo Naledi, New Species in Human Lineage, Is Found in South African Cave".

The Onion's quotation is 3 times longer; it does not just quote Dr. Berger, but also describes his motive and emotional state. The greater number of clauses increases the number of punctuation marks found in satire, which informed the development of our successful *Punctuation* feature. Our *Grammar* feature set incorporates the complexity of phrasing.

5.2. Our Satirical Detection Approach and News Satire Features

Based on previous methodological advances in irony, humor, and satire detection, and our data-

3 The Globe and Mail, The Vancouver Sun, Calgary Herald, National Post, The Edmonton Journal, The Hamilton Spectator, USA Today, The Wall Street Journal, Los Angeles Times, The New York Post, Newsday, and The Denver Post.

4 www.cbc.ca/punchline, thelapine.ca, syruptrap.ca, www.thecodfish.com, urbananomie.com, www.newyorker.com/humor/borowitz-report, dailycurrant.com, www.thespoof.com, nationalreport.net, worldnewsdailyreport.com, and thepeoplescube.com.

5 http://victoriarubin.fims.uwo.ca/news-verification/

driven linguistic observations, we propose and test a set of 5 satirical news features: *Absurdity, Humor, Grammar, Negative Affect* and *Punctuation*. The method begins with performing a topic-based classification followed by sentiment-based classification, and feature selection based on absurdity and humor heuristics. The training and evaluation of our model uses a state-of-the-art method of support vector machines (SVMs) using a 75% training and 25% test split of the dataset, and 10-fold cross validation applied to the training vectors. We combined cross-validation with the holdout method in reporting overall model performance. Cross validation on our 75% training produced a performance prediction on incoming data. We then confirmed this prediction in a second stage using our 25% hold out testing set. This allowed us to investigate which records from the set were incorrectly predicted by the model.

Text Processing and Feature Weighting: The text classification pipeline was scripted in Python 2.7 and used the *scikit-learn* open source machine learning package (Pedregosa et al., 2011) as the primary SVM classification and model evaluation API. In our approach, we described news articles as sparse feature vectors using a topic-based classification methodology with the term frequency-inverse document frequency (tf*idf) weighting scheme. The baseline results for our news corpus was achieved using a linear kernel classifier (Pedregosa et al., 2011) that assigns positive instances to satire. First, news article text was preprocessed, transforming the raw text to a Pandas data structure for use in Python. Stop words were removed, and unigrams and bigrams were tokenized. Both the training and test data were converted to tf-idf feature vectors. Term frequency values were also normalized by article length to account for length variability between satirical and legitimate news articles. The process is implemented as a semi-automated pipeline, summarized in Figure 3.

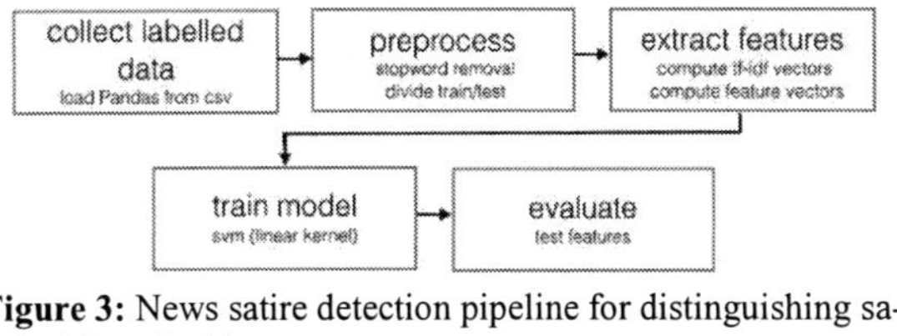

Figure 3: News satire detection pipeline for distinguishing satirical from legitimate news.

Feature Selection: ***The Absurdity Feature (Abs)*** was defined by the unexpected introduction of new named entities (people, places, locations) within the final sentence of satirical news. To implement *Absurdity* detection we used the Natural Language Toolkit[6] (NLTK) Part of Speech tagger and Named Entity Recognizer to detect the list of named entities. We defined the list as the non-empty set (LNE), and compared this with the set (NE) of named entities appearing in the remaining article. The article was deemed absurd when the intersection (LNE ∩ NE) was empty (0=non-absurd, 1=absurd).

Humor (Hum) detection was based on the premises of opposing scripts and maximizing semantic distance between two statements as method of punchline identification (Mihalcea et al., 2010). Similarly, in a humorous article, the lead and final sentence are minimally related. Our modification of the punchline detection method assigned the binary value (humor=1) when the relatedness between the first and last article sentences was the minimum with respect to the remaining sentences.

We used a knowledge-based metric to measure the relatedness between statement pairs in the article and sought to minimize relatedness of the lead and last line. Given a metric for word-to-word relatedness, we define the semantic relatedness of two text segments S1 and S2 using a metric that combines the semantic relatedness of each text segment in turn with respect to the other text segment. For each word *w* in the segment S1 we identified the word in the segment S2 that has the highest semantic relatedness, as per (Wu & Palmer, 1994) word-to-word similarity metric. The depth of two given concepts in the WordNet taxonomy, and the depth of the least common subsumer (LCS) were combined into a similarity score (Wu & Palmer, 1994). The same process was applied to find the most similar word in S1 starting with words in S2. The word similarities were weighted, summed, and normalized with the length of each text segment. The resulting relatedness scores were averaged.

Grammar (Gram) feature vector was the set of normalized term frequencies matched against the Linguistic Inquiry and Word Count (LIWC) 2015 dictionaries, which accounts for the percentage of

6 http://www.nltk.org/

words that reflect different linguistic categories (Pennebaker, Boyd, Jordan, & Blackburn, 2015). We counted the presence of parts of speech terms including adjectives, adverbs, pronouns, conjunctions, and prepositions, and assigned each normalized value as the element in a feature array representing grammar properties.

Negative Affect (Neg) and ***Punctuation (Pun)*** were assigned as feature weights representing normalized frequencies based on term-for-term comparisons with LIWC 2015 dictionaries. Values were assigned based on the presence of negative affect terms and punctuation (periods, comma, colon, semi-colon, question marks, exclamation, quotes) in the training and test set. Features representing *Absurdity, Humor, Grammar, Negative Affect* and *Punctuation* were introduced in succession to train the model, combined overall. The predictive performance was measured at the introduction of each new feature and the best performing features were combined and compared to the overall performance of all 5.

6. Evaluation

We conducted multiple experiments to identify the best-performing combination of features for satirical news identification. We used scikit-learn (Pedregosa et al., 2011) and the *tf*idf* F-measure as the baseline (***Base***, Table 2), with features added incrementally. Scikit-learn library contains several tools designed for machine learning applications in Python[7], and has been utilized in the supervised learning applications of real and fake news detection (Pisarevskaya, 2015; Rubin & Lukoianova, 2014). The *Sklearn.svm* package is a set of supervised learning methods used for classification, regression and outlier detection, capable of performing multi-class classification. We assigned two classes: satirical news (1) and legitimate news (0), and used *Sklearn.svm.SVC* (Support Vector Classification) for supervised training with a linear kernel algorithm, which is suitable for 2 class training data. Our model was trained on 270 and tested on a set of 90 news articles, with equal proportions of satirical and legitimate news. Table 2 presents the measures of precision, recall, and F-score with associated 10-fold cross validation confidence results for our satire detection model. The F-score was maximized in the case when *Grammar, Punctuation* and *Absurdity* features were used. Precision was highest when *Punctuation* and *Grammar* were included. *Absurdity* showed the highest recall performance.

7 http://scikit-learn.org

FEATURES	PRECISION	RECALL	F-SCORE	CONFIDENCE
Base (*tf-idf*)	78	87	82	85
Base+Abs	85	**89**	87	83
Base +Hum	80	87	83	83
Base+Gram	**93**	82	87	82
Base+Neg	81	84	83	84
Base+Pun	**93**	82	87	87
Base+Gram+Pun+Abs	**90**	84	87	84
Base+All	88	82	87	87

Table 2: Satirical news detection evaluation results with 10-fold cross-validation. [**Legend: Base**= baseline tf-idf topic vector; **Abs**= Absurdity [0,1]; Hum= Humor [0,1]; **Gram**= Grammar features (pronoun, preposition, adjective, adverb, conjunction); Neg = Negative Affect; **Pun**= Punctuation; All= all features combined.]

7. Discussion

Our findings produced a set of observations about the benefits of detection methods for satire in news, as well as what methods were not useful and how they can be improved. We were able to integrate word level features using an established machine learning approach in text classification, SVM (Burfoot & Baldwin, 2009), to derive empirical cues indicative to deception. This included establishing a baseline model in the form of tf-idf feature weights, while measuring net effects of additional features against the baseline. Our baseline model performed with 82% accuracy, an improvement on Mihalcea et al. (2010) who achieved a 65% baseline score with tf-idf method on similar input data. Contrary to our expectations, we discovered that individual textual features of shallow syntax (parts of speech) and punctuation marks are highly indicative of the presence of satire, producing a detection improvement of 5% (87% F-score). This suggests that the rhetorical component of satire may provide reliable cues to its identification. Based on our manual analysis, this finding may be due to the presence of more complex sentence structures (prevalence of dependent clauses) in satirical content, and strategic use of run-on sentences for comedic affect. However, this pattern did not translate to longer sentences per se, since our average words-per-sentence feature did not increase predictive accuracy. Also contrary to our expectation, markers such as profanity and slang, word level features deemed significant by Burfoot and Baldwin (2009), produced no measurable improvements in our trials. Our dataset may not have included more extreme examples of satire.

One major contribution of the current research is that we were able to integrate a heuristic for *Absurdity* feature *(Abs,* Table 2*)* derived from the concept of *semantic validity,* the stark and strategic use of mismatched named entities in a story as a comic device. Burfoot and Baldwin's (2009) method of translating search results on co-occurring entities to an absurdity measure informed our approach, when we noticed that satirical sources often introduce previously non-occurring entities in the final sentence. Compared to Burfoot and Baldwin's 65% performance, our results show a 5% improvement (F-score 87%), when we added this feature to our baseline. Our intuition about named entities proved to be a defining empirical feature of satirical news.

Another concept derived from the theoretical literature on humor is the idea of shifting reference frames, and incongruity resolution based on the semantic derivation of textual components. We adapted methods based on identifying latent terms (Sjöbergh and Araki, 2007) in punchline detection against a setup statement. Instead of relying on more complex methods of representing longer text (through TMRs per Hempelmann et al. (2006), we modified the semantic distance approach between the lead sentence (setup) and the last sentence (punchline) which is hypothesized to be maximized in satire. The results of Mihalcea and Pulman (2007) showed a performance of 84% using word-wise semantic distance in WordNet classification. Our model showed a comparable performance of 83% when this feature was added to the baseline, opening up another avenue of extending opposing scripts to a news corpus.

The presence of polarity in satire has been noted in previous methods (Reyes et al., 2013); such as indicated by positive or negative semantic orientation, emotiveness, and emotional words. Our findings partially bolster this conclusion when we demonstrated that features representing negative affect improved the performance to 83% in the identification task. However, we found no similar improvement when we measured the contrasting effect of positive semantic orientation.

8. Conclusions & Future Work

In this paper, we have translated theories of humor, irony, and satire into a predictive method for satire detection that reaches relatively high accuracy rates (90% precision, 84% recall, 87% F-score). Since satirical news is at least part of the time deceptive, identifying satirical news pieces can aid in minimizing the potential deceptive impact of satirical news. By analyzing the current news production landscape captured within our dataset, we demonstrate the feasibility of satire detection methods even when divorced from attribution to a satirical source. Our conceptual contribution is in linking deception detection and computational satire, irony and humor research. Practically, this study frames fake news as a worthy target for filtering due to its potential to mislead news readers. Areas of further investigation can include ways to translate more complex characteristics of the anatomy of satire into linguistic cues. Critique and call to action, combined with mockery, is a key component of satire, but this critical component (II, Ermida, 2012) has not yet received much attention in the field of NLP. This feature could be subject to automated discourse-level quantification through the presence of imperative sentences. Also, our positive results of shallow syntax features showed us that more complex language patterns, for example deep syntax and the ordering of grammatical patterns might also be detectable in satire through techniques such as regular expression pattern matching against a grammatical parse of article content.

Acknowledgments

This research has been funded by the Government of Canada Social Sciences and Humanities Research Council (SSHRC) Insight Grant (#435-2015-0065) awarded to Dr. Rubin for the project *Digital Deception Detection: Identifying Deliberate Misinformation in Online News.*

References

Attardo, S., Hempelmann, C. F., & Mano, S. D. (2002). Script oppositions and logical mechanisms:

Modeling incongruities and their resolutions. *Humor, 15*(1), 3-46.

Buller, D. B., & Burgoon, J. K. (1996). Interpersonal Deception Theory. *Communication Theory, 6*(3), 203-242.

Burfoot, C., & Baldwin, T. (2009). *Automatic satire detection: are you having a laugh?* Paper presented at the Proceedings of the ACL-IJCNLP 2009 Conference Short Papers, Suntec, Singapore.

Chen, Y., Conroy, N. J., & Rubin, V. L. (2015). *News in an online world: the need for an automatic crap detector.* Paper presented at the Proceedings of the 78th ASIS&T Annual Meeting: Information Science with Impact: Research in and for the Community.

Condren, C. (2012). Satire and definition. *Humor, 25*(4), 375. doi:10.1515/humor-2012-0019

Condren, C. (2014). Satire. In S. Attardo (Ed.), *Encyclopedia of Humor Studies*. Thousand Oaks: Sage Publications, Inc.

Davidov, D., Tsur, O., & Rappoport, A. (2010). *Semi-supervised recognition of sarcastic sentences in twitter and amazon.* Paper presented at the Fourteenth Conference on Computational Natural Language Learning, Uppsala, Sweden.

DePaulo, B. M., Charlton, K., Cooper, H., Lindsay, J. J., & Muhlenbruck, L. (1997). The Accuracy-Confidence Correlation in the Detection of Deception. *Personality and Social Psychology Review, 1*(4), 346-357.

Ermida, I. (2012). News Satire in the Press: Linguistic Construction of Humour in Spoof News Articles. In J. Chovanec & I. Ermida (Eds.), *Language and humour in the media*. Newcastle upon Tyne, UK: Cambridge Scholars Pub.

Frye, N. (1944). The Nature of Satire. *University of Toronto Quarterly, 14*(1), 75-89.

Hango, D. (2014). *University graduates with lower levels of literacy and numeracy skills.* Statistics Canada Retrieved from http://www.statcan.gc.ca/pub/75-006-x/2014001 /article/14094-eng.htm.

Hempelmann, C., Raskin, V., & Triezenberg, K. E. (2006). *Computer, Tell Me a Joke... but Please Make it Funny: Computational Humor with Ontological Semantics.* Paper presented at the FLAIRS Conference, Melbourne Beach, Florida, USA.

Highet, G. (1972). *The Anatomy of Satire*. Princeton, N.J: Princeton University Press.

Hongo, H. (2016). Literally Unbelievable: Stories from The Onion as interpreted by Facebook. Retrieved from http://literallyunbelievable.org/

Hopper, R., & Bell, R. A. (1984). Broadening the Deception Construct. *Quarterly Journal of Speech, 70*(3), 288-302.

Howell, L. (2013). *Global Risks 2013*. Retrieved from Cologny/Geneva, Switzerland: http://www3. weforum.org/docs/WEF_GlobalRisks_Report_2013.pdf

LaMarre, H. L., Landreville, K. D., & Beam, M. A. (2009). The Irony of Satire: Political Ideology and the Motivation to See What You Want to See in The Colbert Report. *The International Journal of Press/Politics, 14*(2), 212-231. doi:10.1177/1940161208330904

Mihalcea, R., & Liu, H. (2006). *A corpus-based approach to finding happiness.* Paper presented at the AAAI Symposium on Computational Approaches to Analyzing Weblogs.

Mihalcea, R., & Pulman, S. (2007). Characterizing humour: An exploration of features in humorous texts. In A. Gelbukh (Ed.), *Computational Linguistics and Intelligent Text Processing* (Vol. 4394, pp. 337-347). Berlin Heidelberg: Springer.

Mihalcea, R., Strapparava, C., & Pulman, S. (2010). *Computational models for incongruity detection in humour.* Paper presented at the Computational linguistics and intelligent text processing, Iasi, Romania.

Mocanu, D., Rossi, L., Zhang, Q., Karsai, M., & Quattrociocchi, W. (2015). Collective attention in the age of (mis)information. *Computers in Human Behavior, 51*, 1198-1204. doi:10.1016/j.chb.2015.01.024

Pedregosa, F., Varoquaux, G., Gramfort, A., Michel, V., Thirion, B., Grisel, O., . . . Dubourg, V. (2011). Scikit-learn: Machine learning in Python. *The Journal of Machine Learning Research, 12*, 2825-2830.

Pennebaker, J. W., Boyd, R. L., Jordan, K., & Blackburn, K. (2015). The Development and Psychometric Properties of LIWC2015. from University of Texas at Austin http://hdl.handle.net/2152/31333

Pennycook, G., Cheyne, J. A., Barr, N., Koehler, D. J., & Fugelsang, J. A. (2015). On the reception and detection of pseudo-profound bullshit. *Judgment and Decision Making, 10*(6), 549-563.

Pfaff, K. L., & Gibbs, R. W. (1997). Authorial intentions in understanding satirical texts. *Poetics, 25*(1), 45-70. doi:10.1016/s0304-422x(97)00006-5

Phiddian, R. (2013). Satire and the limits of literary theories. *Critical Quarterly, 55*(3), 44-58.

Pisarevskaya, D. (2015). *Rhetorical Structure Theory as a Feature for Deception Detection in News Reports in the Russian Language.* Paper presented at the Artificial Intelligence and Natural Language & Information Extraction, Social Media and Web Search (AINL-ISMW) FRUCT Conference, Saint-Petersburg, Russia.

Polanyi, L., & Zaenen, A. (2006). Contextual valence shifters. In J. G. Shanahan, Y. Qu, & J. Wiebe (Eds.), *Computing attitude and affect in text: Theory and applications* (1 ed., pp. 1-10): Springer Netherlands.

Reilly, R., & Nye, R. (2012). *Power, principles and the press*. Retrieved from http://www.theopen-road.com/wp-content/uploads/2012/09/Power-principles-and-the-press-Open-Road-and-Populus1.pdf

Reyes, A., & Rosso, P. (2014). On the difficulty of automatically detecting irony: beyond a simple case of negation. *Knowledge and Information Systems, 40*(3), 595-614. doi:10.1007/s10115-013-0652-8

Reyes, A., Rosso, P., & Buscaldi, D. (2012). From humor recognition to irony detection: The figurative language of social media. *Data & Knowledge Engineering, 74*, 1-12. doi:10.1016/j.datak.2012.02.005

Reyes, A., Rosso, P., & Veale, T. (2013). A multidimensional approach for detecting irony in Twitter. *Language Resources and Evaluation, 47*(1), 239-268. doi:10.1007/s10579-012-9196-x

Riffkin, R. (2015, 2015/09/28/). Americans' Trust in Media Remains at Historical Low. *Gallup*. Retrieved from http://www.gallup.com/poll/185927/americans-trust-media-remains-historical-low.aspx

Rubin, V. L., Chen, Y., & Conroy, N. J. (2015). *Deception detection for news: three types of fakes.* Paper presented at the Proceedings of the 78th ASIS&T Annual Meeting: Information Science with Impact: Research in and for the Community.

Rubin, V. L., & Conroy, N. (2012). Discerning truth from deception: Human judgments and automation efforts. *First Monday, 17*(3). Retrieved from http://firstmonday.org/ojs/index.php/fm/article/view/3933/3170

Rubin, V. L., & Lukoianova, T. (2014). Truth and Deception at the Rhetorical Structure Level. *Journal of the Association for Information Science and Technology, 66*(5), 12. doi:10.1002/asi.23216

Simpson, P. (2003). *On the Discourse of Satire*: John Benjamins Publishing Company.

Sjöbergh, J., & Araki, K. (2007). *Recognizing humor without recognizing meaning.* Paper presented at the International Workshop on Fuzzy Logic and Applications, Camogli, Italy.

The Media Insight Project. (2014). *The rational and attentive news consumer*. Retrieved from https://www.americanpressinstitute.org/publications/reports/survey-research/rational-attentive-news-consumer/

Tsfati, Y. (2010). Online News Exposure and Trust in the Mainstream Media: Exploring Possible Associations. *American Behavioral Scientist, 54*(1), 22-42. doi:10.1177/0002764210376309

Tsur, O., Davidov, D., & Rappoport, A. (2010, May 23-26 2010). *ICWSM — A Great Catchy Name: Semi-Supervised Recognition of Sarcastic Sentences in Online Product Reviews.* Paper presented at the Fourth International AAAI Conference on Web and Social Media, George Washington University, Washington, D.C. USA.

Utsumi, A. (2000). Verbal irony as implicit display of ironic environment: Distinguishing ironic utterances from nonirony. *Journal of Pragmatics, 32*(12), 1777-1806. doi:http://dx.doi.org/10.1016/S0378-2166(99)00116-2

Van Swol, L. (2014). Truth Bias. In T. Levine (Ed.), *Encyclopedia of Deception* (Vol. 1, pp. 904-906). Thousand Oaks, California: SAGE Publications.

Vrij, A., Mann, S., & Leal, S. (2012). Deception Traits in Psychological Interviewing. *Journal of Police and Criminal Psychology, 28*(2), 115-126.

Wu, Z., & Palmer, M. (1994). *Verbs semantics and lexical selection.* Paper presented at the 32nd Annual Meeting of the Association for Computational Linguistics, Las Cruces, New Mexico.

Zhou, L., Burgoon, J. K., Nunamaker, J. F., & Twitchell, D. (2004). Automating Linguistics-Based Cues for Detecting Deception in Text-Based Asynchronous Computer-Mediated Communications. *Group Decision and Negotiation, 13*(1), 81-106.

Ziv, A. (1988). Teaching and Learning with Humor. *The Journal of Experimental Education, 57*(1), 4-15. doi:10.1080/00220973.1988.10806492

Using the verifiability of details as a test of deception: A conceptual framework for the automation of the verifiability approach

Bennett Kleinberg[1], Galit Nahari[2] and Bruno Verschuere[1]
[1] Department of Psychology, University of Amsterdam, The Netherlands.
[2] Department of Criminology, Bar-Ilan University, Ramat Gan, Israel.
{b.a.r.kleinberg,b.j.verschuere}@uva.nl galit.nahari@biu.ac.il

Abstract

The Verifiability Approach (VA) is a promising new approach for deception detection. It extends existing verbal credibility assessment tools by asking interviewees to provide statements rich in verifiable detail. Details that *i)* have been experienced with an identifiable person, *ii)* have been witnessed by an identifiable person, or *iii)* have been recorded through technology, are labelled as verifiable. With only minimal modifications of information-gathering interviews this approach has yielded remarkable classification accuracies. Currently, the VA relies on extensive manual annotation by human coders. Aiming to extend the VA's applicability, we present a work in progress on automated VA scoring. We provide a conceptual outline of two automation approaches: one being based on the *Linguistic Inquiry and Word Count* software and the other on rule-based shallow parsing and named entity recognition. Differences between both approaches and possible future steps for an automated VA are discussed.

1 Cognitive deception detection

Based on the rationale that the default setting in human communication is honesty (Levine, 2014; Verschuere & Shalvi, 2014), the cognitive approach to deception (e.g. Zuckerman et al., 1981) postulates that the act of lying requires extra mental effort compared to telling the truth (e.g. trying to fabricate a convincing lie; Vrij, 2014). The general idea of lying being correlated to increased mental effort has been corroborated by a great body of research, using self-reports, behavioral, autonomic, electrophysiological, and neural measures (Ganis et al., 2003; Verschuere et al., 2011). To further increase cognitive differences between lying and truth telling, the cognitive approach advocates applying minimal interventions in information-gathering interviewing situations that enlarge the differences between the truth tellers and liars (e.g. asking unexpected questions, asking to recall a story in reverse order; Vrij et al., 2015, Meissner et al., 2012). A recent meta-analysis indicates that cognitive techniques outperform standard interviews (Vrij et al., 2015). This body of work has also found the most reliable differences between truths and lies to be manifested in verbal rather than nonverbal behavior. Ormerod and Dando (2014), for instance, applied cognitive interviewing techniques on mock-passengers and found verbal detection methods to by far outperform its behavioral counterparts (e.g. spotting suspicious behavior). Also, objective judgments (i.e., algorithmic scoring such as discriminant analysis) outperformed human judgments (truths: 60% vs. 80%; lies: 64% vs. 73%, for human vs. objective judgments, respectively, Vrij et al., 2015). The superiority of objective criteria might be explained by the sheer amount of information for humans to take into account to derive a binary truth versus lie judgment (e.g. Rubin & Conroy, 2012).

Proceedings of NAACL-HLT 2016, pages 18–25,
San Diego, California, June 12-17, 2016. ©2016 Association for Computational Linguistics

The verbal content of statements seems to offer potential for cognition-based deception detection. Verbal deception detection offers multiple levels of analysis (e.g. overall content of statements, lexical analysis, syntactic analysis, see Fitzpatrick et al., 2015) and the most promising results of deception research fall under the umbrella term of verbal deception detection (e.g. Ott et al., 2011, 2013; Mihalcea et al., 2013; Harvey et al., 2016). Unlike other approaches, verbal deception detection is suitable for large-scale applications due to its potential for computer-automation. The cognitive approach to increasing the differences between liars and truth tellers provides a theoretical framework for a synthesis of computer-automated approaches and validated information-gathering interviewing techniques.

2 The Verifiability Approach

2.1 Rationale

Information gathering interviews typically ask the interviewee for a detailed account of the events (e.g. *"Describe in as much detail as possible what happened"*). Derived bottom-up from the liars' verbal strategies (Nahari et al., 2014a), the Verifiability Approach (VA) aims to further increase the differences between liars and truth tellers. The VA is based on three assumptions about the liars' dilemma in an interview:

(1) Liars are inclined to mention sufficient details to provide a convincing false account.
(2) Liars try to avoid mentioning those details that can potentially be verified by the interviewer.
(3) As solution to (1) and (2), the liars provide many *non-verifiable details*.

Working from this dilemma, Nahari et al. (2014a) developed a set of criteria deemed appropriate as an indication of the verifiability of a detail given in a statement. Specifically, a detail is categorized as verifiable if at least one of the three criteria below applies:

- The detail describes an activity with an identifiable person.
- The detail describes an activity that has been witnessed by an identifiable person.
- The detail describes an activity that may have been documented or recorded through technology.

Type of detail	Example
Verifiable detail	*"My husband and I parked the car outside our house and noticed our neighbour's daughter kissing her boyfriend good-bye on their doorstep."* [with an identifiable person] *"There were 3 people present who witnessed me use my phone before placing it in my bag at 22:00: Ben Kleinberg, Galit Nahari, and Bruno Verschuere."* (names changed) [witnessed by an identifiable person] *"My phone was last used at 12.30 am in which I sent a text message to my friend who was with me that evening."* [recorded through technology]
Non-verifiable detail	*"When I got back to my house I realised that my phone was no longer in my pocket, but had gone."* *"I spoke to a lady in the shop about the general chit chat of an airport, where she was going to and when her flight was."* *"A guy offered to buy me a drink after noticing it was my birthday."*

Table 1: Illustration of verifiable (criterion in square brackets) and non-verifiable details (verbatim from Vrij et al., 2016).

Table 1 shows verbatim examples for each category from the most recent VA study (Vrij et al., 2016).

2.2 Verifiable details and verifiable facts

Hancock et al. (2005) outline that liars use more details when the nature of the deception permits it (i.e., when the narrative *per se* is non-verifiable). For example, opinions are inherently non-verifiable fact

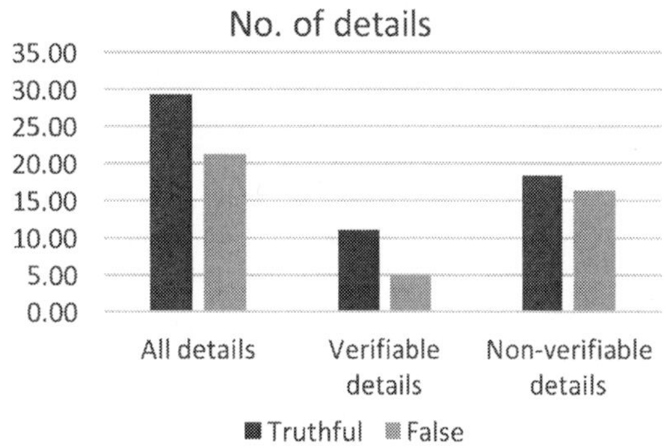

Figure 1: Number of details per category and condition in Nahari et al. (2014a).

scenarios. In contrast, event-based deception settings like mock-crimes are verifiable fact scenarios. In this sense, verifiable facts are interwoven with the ground truth of a deception study: established ground truth provides verifiable facts for the researcher regarding the narrative, and vice versa.

Interestingly, this important distinction between verifiable and non-verifiable facts made by Hancock et al. (2005, 2007), is relevant to the VA in two ways: First, the application of the VA is appropriate only when the scenario is based on theoretically verifiable facts (e.g., a crime). In its current state, the VA is less relevant for non-verifiable fact scenarios (e.g., opinions), as one cannot verify details that are not event-based. Second, Hancock et al. (2005) discuss how liars' verbosity could depend on the verifiability of the overall scenario. In situations where the verifiability or ground truth is difficult to establish (e.g. opinions), the liars may choose to include many details in their statement, whereas this strategy is expected to be counterproductive when the ground truth can be established. The VA extends this idea by actively challenging interviewees in different ways: liars and truth tellers are explicitly asked to provide verifiable details. This technique results in a disproportionally difficult task for the liars, whereas the truth teller can easily recall verifiable details from memory.

3 Experimental findings using the VA

In the initial experiment on the VA, Nahari et al. (2014a) modified a mock-crime procedure by instructing participants to do their normal daily business (e.g. drinking coffee, visiting a book shop) and return to the lab after 30 minutes. Upon returning to the lab, the participants were allocated to the truth-condition or the lie-condition. Those in the truth-condition were instructed to provide a truthful account of their activities in the previous 30 minutes, whereas those in the lie-condition were required to give an entirely false statement. The findings (Figure 1) show that truthful statements contained more overall details ($p < .05$) as a function of the number of verifiable details ($p < .001$). Moreover, the number of details translated to promising classification rates (Table 2). These general findings have been corroborated in several studies (e.g. Nahari & Vrij, 2014; Nahari & Vrij, 2015).

	F-measure true statements	**F-measure false statements**	**Accuracy**
No. of verifiable details	80.95	76.47	78.94
No. of all details	69.57	53.33	63.16
No. of verifiable details/no. of non-verifiable details	73.17	68.57	71.05

Table 2: F-measures and accuracies of the VA for three decision criteria (from Nahari et al., 2014a)

From a methodological point of view, two essential elements in this study are the annotation of details in statements and subsequently the annotation of these details as either verifiable or non-verifiable.

3.1 Annotation of details

In order to extract details from the statements written by the participants, the researchers adopted the Reality Monitoring approach (RM; Sporer, 2004). RM has gained popularity in deception research because it offers a theoretical framework about content differences of true and false statements (Johnson & Raye, 1981; Vrij, 2015). The underlying assumption of RM is that true experiences are obtained through perceptual processes whereas imagined (or false) experiences are obtained through cognitive operations. This in turn is thought to be reflected in, for example, the amount and type of detail when recalling an experience. Specifically, three of the eight RM criteria are suitable for a verifiability approach (see Nahari et al., 2014a): spatial (e.g. locations or spatial arrangements), temporal (e.g. points in time or sequence of events), and perceptual details (e.g. all sensorial information like visual information and sounds), all which truth tellers are expected to produce more of.

In Nahari et al. (2014a) two independent coders were trained in coding example statements on the three detail criteria for 2.5 hours. Within each statement, the two coders manually annotated all details that were spatial, temporal or perceptual, with an inter-rater reliability of 78%, 77%, and 78%, for perceptual, spatial and temporal details respectively. If the two coders disagreed, a third trained coder made the final decision about the presence of a detail. Consider two examples from Table 1 as illustration:

a) "My husband and I parked the car outside our house and noticed our neighbour's daughter kissing her boyfriend good bye on their doorstep."

b) *"When I got back to my house I realised that my phone was no longer in my pocket, but had gone"*

These statements are annotated as:

a) "My husband [PERCEPTUAL] *and I* parked [PERCEPTUAL] *the car* outside our house [SPATIAL] *and* noticed our neighbour's daughter [PERCEPTUAL] kissing her boyfriend [PERCEPTUAL] *good-bye* on their doorstep [SPATIAL]."

b) "When [TEMPORAL] *I got back to* my house [SPATIAL] *I realised that my phone was no longer in my pocket, but had gone"*

Within this statement, all details that fit one of the three RM criteria are annotated. The next step in the annotation is to decide for each detail whether or not it can be deemed potentially verifiable.

3.2 Annotation of the verifiability of details

The annotated details were further classified as verifiable or non-verifiable (Table 1). Similar to the detail annotation, the same two independent coders made a judgment for each detail whether it fit at least one of the three verifiability criteria (see 2.1). The coders agreed on 87.95% of the detail verifiability (Nahari et al., 2014a). Each disagreement was referred to a third coder who made the final decision. After this final annotation, the overall number of details and of verifiable details was subjected to a discriminant analysis. Applied to the two examples, this phase would result in the following annotation:

a) "My husband [PERC.-VERIFIABLE] *and I* parked [PERC.-VERIFIABLE] *the car* outside our house [SPATIAL-VERIFIABLE] *and* noticed our neighbour's daughter [PERC.-VERIFIABLE] kissing her boyfriend [PERC.-VERIFIABLE] *good-bye* on their doorstep [SPATIAL-VERIFIABLE]."

b) "When [TEMP.-NONVERIFIABLE] *I got back to* my house [SPATIAL-NONVERIFIABLE] *I realised that my phone was no longer in my pocket, but had gone"*

3.3 The VA information protocol

Despite the promising initial results, a key challenge to the VA is that liars can embed their lies into mainly true events, e.g., their normal daily routine (Nahari et al., 2014b), or altogether within non-verifiable scenarios (Hancock et al., 2005). For example, when using the VA on participants' statements about false and true insurance claims, initial findings indicated that the VA does not benefit when the lies are embedded in mainly non-verifiable contexts. However, contrary to other content analysis tools (Nahari & Pazualo, 2015) the VA has been shown to allow for higher classification accuracy when the participants were aware of the working mechanisms of the tool. Harvey et al. (2016) manipulated the information liars and truth tellers received about the VA in the insurance claim setting: one group in each condition (truth vs. lie) was told to provide as much detail as possible whereas another group was informed that verifiable details are used as an indicator for truthfulness. The accuracy in the informed group (77.5%) was higher than that in the uninformed group (57.5%). This information protocol manipulation affected liars and truth tellers in

	Detail annotation	Verifiability annotation
Human coding	Manually	Manually
LIWC-based system	Word frequencies of 'perceptual processes', 'space', and 'time'	*Unlikely to be captured*
NER-based system	Shallow parsing of verb phrases	Presence of named entities as proxy for verifiability

Table 3: Conceptual comparison of VA automation approaches.

unequal ways (see 2.2) and it has now become standard procedure in VA research.

3.4 Towards large scale application of VA

Although the VA has yielded promising results in laboratory studies it is limited with regard to its large-scale applicability. Most importantly, the annotation of details and verifiability relies on manual coding making this procedure resource-intensive (e.g. Harvey et al., 2016). In other words, the manual coding of verbal criteria can be seen as a key impediment to large-scale investigations with the VA and potential applications. In the remainder of this paper, we report on a work in progress about the automation of the VA.

4 Related work on automated verbal deception detection

To put our work into perspective we briefly discuss three key studies on automated approaches to verbal deception detection. Zhou et al. (2004) conducted one of the early experimental attempts to automate the detection of deception in a computer-mediated communication eliciting lies in a group decision problem. Crucially, they found that computerized analysis added significantly to the identification of linguistic cues for the detection of deception in asynchronous settings. Mihalcea et al. (2013) answer another relevant question for the broader aim of this investigation. They showed that a data-driven machine learning approach achieved classification accuracies of up to 74% for low-stakes lies (see also Mihalcea & Strappavara, 2009). A study by Bachenko et al. (2008) complements this finding by addressing the critical issue of low-stakes with a linguistic analysis of genuine crime documents. On the one hand, they showed that a theory-based selection of cues can successfully be automated for linguistic annotation of texts, and on the other hand, they were able to develop a tagging system that discriminated true from false declaration within statements. The latter is of particular relevance for the problem of embedded lies.

5 Automating the VA

The main research question guiding this conceptual paper is whether we can automate the VA. As this is the first automated annotation approach of the VA, we will use the data of existing VA studies (e.g. Nahari et al., 2014a; Vrij et al., 2016) which will both be readily available and provide human scoring as baseline. We discuss two automation approaches that could both address the annotation of details but differ in their potential of annotating the verifiability. The first system is based on the *Linguistic Inquiry and Word Count* system (LIWC, Pennebaker et al., 2015) and the second system is a two-phasic annotation approach relying on named entity recognition.

5.1 LIWC-based automation

The LIWC system (Pennebaker et al., 2015) has been applied widely in psycholinguistic research (e.g. Bond & Lee, 2005; Hancock et al., 2007; Ramirez-Esparza et al., 2008). The software analyzes text statements and produces frequency tables of word categories that fit psychological processes (e.g. cognitive mechanism, affect). Bond and Lee (2005) applied LIWC to automate RM criteria in a sample of prisoners. We aim to adopt their approach to modelling the VA detail categories (perceptual, spatial, temporal) with the LIWC word categories 'perceptual processes' (e.g., "saw", "heard"), 'space' (e.g., "down", "under"), and 'time' (e.g., "before", "until"). We will use the frequency of these word categories as proxy for overall detail in existing statements from VA studies (Table 3). Whereas we expect the annotation of details to be feasible in this system (see Bond & Lee, 2015), we argue that the verifiability is less likely to be captured. The current LIWC system does not provide a word category or output that we think is able to function as proxy for detail verifiability.

5.2 Shallow parsing and NER system

In the second automation approach, we aim to develop a system adopting essentially rule-based shallow parsing (Pradhan et al., 2004) of statement activities and details that will then be coupled with *named entity recognition* (NER; e.g. persons, locations, organizations; Weischedel et al., 2013; Honnibal, 2016; see Appendix A). Specifically, in this first automation attempt, we aim to use the existing VA data and perform part-of-speech tag rule-based shallow parsing to annotate verb phrases as proxy for activities.

As a second step, we add the verifiability annotation using NER. By extracting named entities, we hypothesize to be able to add significantly to the verifiability annotation as compared to the LIWC-based system. It could be possible that the presence of named entities comes close to fulfilling the actual verifiability criteria (i.e., presence of or witnessing by an identifiable person and reference to technology). For example, the statements "I saw a guy in a cafe" contains no named entity, whereas "I saw Dan in the Starbucks" contains two named entities (Dan = PERSON, Starbucks = ORGANIZATION). Note how in both cases, LIWC and the shallow parser would identify the same detail ("saw"), but only the NER-based system would also annotate the two additional named entities. We will investigate whether the NER-added information functions as a proxy for verifiability. We aim to use Cython-based *spaCy* (Honnibal, 2016) software for pre-processing and annotation. The tokenizer, POS-tagger and NER algorithms are trained on the OntoNotes5 corpus (Weischedel et al., 2013).

6 Outlook and conclusion

The conceptual approach to an automation of the VA is thought to eventually enable large-scale applications. Given the novelty of the VA, the approach to its automation is still in its infancy and requires multiple phases of development. For example, it could be that the LIWC-based system and the NER-approach are not mutually exclusive but that both complement each other. A successful automation of the VA could open up new directions of verbal deception research. First, it would enable researchers to conduct VA experiments on large sample sizes and corpora sizes efficiently. Second, an automated VA could have considerable impact on applied deception research. Especially in the area of crime prevention, the practitioners' focus is identifying the few persons out of a large population who may have false intentions. Inherent to such aims is the need for large-scale automated deception detection tools. Third, on a psycholinguistic level, the VA adds an interesting dimension to scoring mechanisms by explicitly looking at the verifiability of details. Future directions could, for example, involve modifications of the VA as a tool to identify propositions subject to ground truth checking or applying the VA to smaller units of analysis like single propositions instead of whole statements. The latter could also be a step towards detecting embedded lies.

In summary, the VA offers a promising framework for the detection of verbal deception and would benefit from automation. Two approaches were outlined, one based on the LIWC software tool and another based on named entity recognition algorithms. Successfully automated approaches of the VA could contribute to novel research paths and to further integration of cognitive deception detection and computational linguistics.

Acknowledgments

This work is supported by a grant from the Dutch Ministry of Security and Justice. We thank three critical and attentive reviewers and the editor for their invaluable input.

References

Bachenko, J., Fitzpatrick, E., & Schonwetter, M. (2008). Verification and implementation of language-based deception indicators in civil and criminal narratives. *Proceedings of the 22nd International Conference on Computational Linguistics*, 41-48.

Bond, G.B., & Lee, A.Y. (2005). Language of lies in prison: Linguistic classification of prisoners' truthful and deceptive natural language. *Applied Cognitive Psychology, 19*, 313-329. doi:10.1002/acp.1087

Fitzpatrick, E., Bachenko, J., Fornaciari (2015). *Automatic detection of verbal deception*. Morgan & Claypool Publishers.

Ganis, G., Kosslyn, S.M., Stose, S., Thomposon, W.L., & Yurgelun-Todd, D.A. (2003). Neural correlates of different types of deception: An fMRI investigation. *Cerebral Cortex, 13*(8), 830-836. doi: 10.1093/cercor/13.8.830

Hancock, J.T., Curry, L.E., Goorha, S., & Woodworth, M. (2007). On lying and being lied to: A linguistic analysis of deception in computer-mediated communication. *Discourse Processes, 45*(1), 1-23, doi: 10.1080/01638530701739181

Hancock, J.T., Curry, L., Goorha, S., Woodworth, M. (2005). Automated linguistic analysis of deceptive and truthful synchronous computer-mediated communication. *Proceedings of the 38th Hawaii International Conference on System Sciences*, 1-10.

Harvey, A. C., Vrij, A., Nahari, G., & Ludwig, K. (2016). Applying the Verifiability Approach to insurance claims settings: Exploring the effect of the information protocol. *Legal and Criminological Psychology*, n/a–n/a. doi:10.1111/lcrp.12092

Honnibal, M. (2016). spaCy (Version 0.100.6) [Computer software]. Available from https://spacy.io/

Johnson, M. K., & Raye, C. L. (1981). Reality monitoring. *Psychological Review, 88*, 67–85. Retrieved from http://www.apa.org/pubs/journals/rev/index.aspx

Levine, T. R. (2014). Truth-Default Theory (TDT): A theory of human deception and deception detection. *Journal of Language and Social Psychology, 33*(4), 378–392. doi:10.1177/0261927X14535916

Meissner, C.A., Redlich, A.D., Bhatt, S., & Brandon, S. (2012). Interview and interrogation methods and their effects on true and false confessions. Campbell Systematic Reviews, 13. Doi: 10.4073/csr.2012.13

Mihalcea, R., & Strapparava, C. (2009). The lie detector: Explorations in the automatic recognition of deceptive language. *In Proceedings of the Association for Computational Linguistics*, 309-312.

Mihalcea, R., Perez-Rosas, V., & Burzo, M. (2013). Automatic detection of deceit in verbal communication. *Proceedings of the 15th ACM on International conference on multimodal interaction*, 131-134.

Nahari, G., & Vrij, A. (2014). Can I borrow your alibi? The applicability of the verifiability approach to the case of an alibi witness. *Journal of Applied Research in Memory and Cognition, 3*(2), 89–94. doi:10.1016/j.jarmac.2014.04.005

Nahari, G., & Vrij, A. (2015). Can someone fabricate verifiable details when planning in advance? It all depends on the crime scenario. *Psychology, Crime & Law, 21*(10), 987–999. doi:10.1080/1068316X.2015.1077248

Nahari, G., Vrij, A., & Fisher, R. P. (2014a). Exploiting liars' verbal strategies by examining the verifiability of details. *Legal and Criminological Psychology, 19*(2), 227–239. doi:10.1111/j.2044-8333.2012.02069.x

Nahari, G., Vrij, A., & Fisher, R. P. (2014b). The verifiability approach: Countermeasures facilitate its ability to discriminate between truths and lies. *Applied Cognitive Psychology, 28*(1), 122–128. doi:10.1002/acp.2974

Ormerod, T. C., & Dando, C. J. (2014). Finding a Needle in a Haystack: Toward a Psychologically Informed Method for Aviation Security Screening. *Journal of Experimental Psychology: General, 144*(1), 76–84. doi:10.1037xge0000030

Ott, M., Cardie, C., & Hancock, J.T. (2013). Negative deceptive opinion spam. *Proceedings of NAACL-HLT 2013*, 497–501.

Ott, M., Choi, Y., Cardie, C., & Hancock, J.T. (2011). Finding deceptive opinion spam by any stretch of the imagination. *Proceedings of the 49th Annual Meeting of the Association for Computational Linguistics*, 309-319.

Pennebaker, J.W., Booth, R.J., Boyd, R.L., & Francis, M.E. (2015). *Linguistic Inquiry and Word Count: LIWC2015*. Austin, TX: Pennebaker Conglomerates (www.liwc.net).

Pradhan, S., Ward, W., Hacioglu, K., Martin, J.H., & Jurafsky, D. (2004). Shallow semantic parsing using support vector machines. *Proceedings of the Human Language Technology - North American Association for Computational Linguistics*.

Ramirez-Esparza, N., Chung, C.K., Kacewicz, E., & Pennebaker, J.W. (2008). The psychology of word use in depression forums in English and in Spanish: Testing two text analytic approaches. *Association for the Advancement of Artificial Intelligence*, 102-108.

Rubin, V.L., & Conroy, N. (2012). Discerning truth from deception: Human judgments and automation efforts. *First Monday, 17*(3). doi: 10.5210/fm.v17i3.3933

Sporer, S. L. (2004). Reality monitoring and detection of deception. In P. A. Granhag & L. A. Stromwall (Eds.), *The detection of deception in forensic contexts* (pp. 64–102). Cambridge, UK: Cambridge University Press.

Verschuere, B., Ben-Shakhar, G., & Meijer, E. (2011). *Memory detection: theory and application of the Concealed Information Test.* Cambridge, U.K.: Cambridge University Press.

Verschuere, B., & Shalvi, S. (2014). The truth comes out naturally! Does it? *Journal of Language and Social Psychology, 33*, 417-423.

Vrij, A. (2014). Interviewing to detect deception. *European Psychologist, 19,* 184–195. doi:10.1027/1016-9040 a000201

Vrij, A. (2015). Verbal lie detection tools: Statement Validity Analysis, Reality Monitoring and Scientific Content Analysis. In: P.A. Granhag, A. Vrij, and B. Verschuere (Eds.), *Detecting Deception: Current Challenges and Cognitive Approaches*, John Wiley & Sons.

Vrij, A., Fisher, R. P., & Blank, H. (2015). A cognitive approach to lie detection: A meta-analysis. *Legal and Criminological Psychology*, 1–21. doi:10.1111/lcrp.12088

Vrij, A., Nahari, G., Isitt, R., & Leal, S. (2016). Using the verifiability lie detection approach in an insurance claim setting. *Journal of Investigative Psychology and Offender Profiling* (Early view). Doi: 10.1002/jip.1458

Weischedel, R., Palmer, M., Marcus, M., Hovy, E., Pradhan, S., Ramshaw, L., Xue, N., Taylor, A., Kaufman, J., Franchini, M., El-Bachouti, M., Belvin, R., & Houston, A. (2013). *OntoNotes Release 5.0* LDC2013T19. Web Download. Philadelphia: Linguistic Data Consortium, 2013. Retrieved from https://catalog.ldc.upenn.edu/LDC2013T19.

Zhou, L., Burgoon, J., Nunamaker, J., & Twitchell, D. (2004). Automating linguistics-based cues for detecting deception in text-based asynchronous computer-mediated communication. *Group Decision and Negotiation, 13*, 81-106.

Zuckerman, M., DePaulo, B. M., & Rosenthal, R. (1981). Verbal and nonverbal communication of deception. In L. Berkowitz (Ed.), *Advances in experimental social psychology*. New York, NY: Academic Press.

Appendix A

Entities as recognized by spaCy NER algorithm (adopted from https://spacy.io/docs#annotation; most relevant categories in bold):

- **PERSON** (e.g. Bill Gates)
- NORP (nationalities or religious groups)
- **FACILITY** (e.g. Heathrow Airport)
- **ORG** (organization, e.g. Starbucks)
- **GPE** (countries, states, cities)
- **LOC** (locations other than GPE)
- PRODUCT (e.g. vehicles, food)
- **EVENT** (e.g. wars, sports events)
- WORK_OF_ART (title of books, songs)
- LAW (named documents made into laws)
- LANGUAGE (any named language)
- **DATE** (e.g. last week)
- **TIME** (e.g. for 2 hours)
- PERCENT (e.g. 85%)
- QUANTITY (e.g. 15kg, 42km)
- ORDINAL (e.g. first, second, 15th)
- CARDINAL (other numerals)

Estimating the Amenability of New Domains for Deception Detection

Eileen Fitzpatrick
Montclair State University
Montclair NJ 07043
fitzpatricke@mail.montclair.edu

Joan Bachenko
Linguistech LLC
Oxford NJ 07863
jbachenko@linguistech.com

Abstract

In this paper we present an initial experiment in the estimation of the amenability of new domains to true/false classification. We choose four domains, two of which have been classified for deception, and use the out-of-rank distance measure on *n*-grams to aid in deciding whether the third and fourth domains are amenable to T/F classification. We then use a classifier covered in the literature to train on the verified domains and test on the new domains to determine whether the relative distance measure can be a predictor of classification accuracy.

1 Introduction

Recent research in natural language processing has supported the notion that verbal behavior can differentiate truthful from deceptive narratives in several domains, including

- spoken personal narratives [Newman et al. 2003; Mihalcea and Strapparava 2009]
- online hotel reviews [Ott et al., 2011, 2013; Hernandez-Fusilier, 2014; Feng et al., 2012; Feng and Hirst, 2013]
- online book reviews [Fornaciari and Poesio, 2014]
- spoken and written criminal narratives [Bachenko et al., 2008; Fornaciari and Poesio, 2011]
- CEO quarterly conference calls [Larcker and Zakolyukina, 2012]
- emailed cooperative task completion [Zhou, 2004]

These studies result in accuracy rates at predicting True versus False of 70% to 90%. The question we address here is whether an approach similar to this recent work can perform equally successfully across different language domains.

Each study, with the exception of subsequent studies of the online hotel reviews, has built a new data set to analyze its particular domain. Each of these data sets comes at more than typical cost for NLP applications because of the necessity of establishing the truth or falsity of the claim(s) in the data – the "ground truth," either through fact-checking or laboratory experiment – in addition to assembling the narrative data itself.

However, might there be similarities in the language of lies across these various domains? There is a substantial literature in psychology and criminal justice that views false narratives as sharing characteristics in common because they describe imagined rather than real events and attitudes. Criteria-based content analysis [Steller and Kohnken 1989] and Reality Monitoring [Johnson and Raye 1981; Sporer 2004], used in some European courts, rely on such differences, and [Rayson et al. 2001] find differences in parts-of-speech in imaginative as opposed to informative language, for which [Ott et al. 2011] finds corroboration in the false vs. true hotel reviews. So, while we would certainly expect content word choice to depend on the domain,

Proceedings of NAACL-HLT 2016, pages 26–31,
San Diego, California, June 12-17, 2016. ©2016 Association for Computational Linguistics

there may be broader characteristics of the narrative that we could capitalize on that might capture deception in a variety of domains. If so, could we create tools to estimate the difficulty of differentiating deceptive from truthful statements in a new domain based on what we know about this differentiation in previously analyzed domains?

This paper examines the ability of data from known domains to predict the difficulty of adapting a T/F classifier to a new domain. To do this, we apply the out-of-rank distance metric on the most frequently occurring words in four domains, two related to each other and two unrelated, as a measure of domain distance in order to estimate how difficult it would be to adapt a classifier to the new domain. We then test a classifier on the four domains in order to learn whether the distance measure has predicted whether the domains are close enough to be successfully classified for veracity and included in a growing corpus of T/F data.

2 Related Work

Two studies have examined the ability of a classifier trained on one set of data to classify data from a different set.

Newman et al. (2003), using five data sets -- including a spoken narrative about a friend, a spoken defense in a mock crime, and personal opinion narratives on abortion that were either spoken, written, or typed – built six classifiers, training with four data sets and testing on the fifth as well as training and testing interalia among the five. The classification of the mock crime achieved the lowest accuracy (48%) and the written abortion achieved the highest (67%). Subjectively, this is not surprising since the mock crime shared only its spoken mode with one other dataset while the written abortion narrative shared the topic with two others.

Mihalcea and Strapparava's basic 2009 study examined the extent to which 300 false narratives could be distinguished from 300 true narratives on three topics: abortion, the death penalty, and a best friend, with an SVM classifier predicting the t/f distribution of the best friend narratives achieving the best accuracy (77%). In addition, they tested across topics, training on two and testing on the third, with a Naïve Bayes classifier achieving the best accuracy (62%) on the topic of abortion.

Given that the baseline for these early studies was the random performance of human judgments, these accuracy rates support the technique of cross-topic and cross-mode classification, if not cross-domain.

This work represents the extent to which known datasets sharing many common characteristics are similar. But what if we are asked to include a new domain, as yet unmarked for ground truth, in a corpus? Can we estimate the success of porting a classifier built for data with known characteristics to unknown data, prior to committing to the expensive task of establishing ground truth for the new domain? At present, most estimates are based on subjective judgment of the closeness between two data sets. To our knowledge, there has been no formal distance measure that might give empirical support to the feeling that two domains are just too dissimilar to be analyzed by the same classifier.

3 Data Sets

Given two domains, we may have *a priori* judgments about the closeness of their linguistic relationship. Yet, in the areas to which NLP research has been applied to deception, there are many variables that may affect this judgment: the formal language of a legal deposition is different from that of a police interview, and a Facebook post is different from a face-to-face conversation. For this preliminary test of the distance among domains, we chose four domains. Table 1 shows the domains and their characteristics.

	D1	D2	D3	D4
topic	fraud	theft	review	murder
mode	spoken	spoken	written	spoken
register	formal	casual	casual	casual
stakes	high	moderate	low	high
narrator	1	1	many	1
venue	public forum	face-to-face interview	online opinion	face-to-face interview

Table 1: Characteristics of the domains under comparison.

Three, D1, D2, and D4, appear broadly related by topic, criminal justice, and by several other characteristics in the table. All four have been annotated for ground truth, but with D4 showing minimal deceptive behavior, with only four claims identified as lies in 13,581 words, and two of the four claims being single word utterances. We hope to find a metric that would distinguish narratives like that of D4 as not amenable to automatic classification in order to avoid expensive ground truth tagging on a document that will not yield useful results with respect to deception detection.

4 Experimental Setup and Results

4.1 Measuring Domain Distance

As a distance metric, we use the n-gram-based out-of-rank model of Cavnar and Trenkle (1994). We are trying to take advantage of the assumed differences not only in word choice but also in style between the truth teller and the liar, which rules out the more standard distance metric for documents, the vector space model. The term matching used by this model is effective when measuring topic distance, but in most cases, the terms that occur with a given topic will not aid in distinguishing true from false claims, particularly if the terms are limited to content words, which are effective in topic classification but not in identifying differences in style.

For Cavnar and Trenkle, working in text classification, the out-of-rank measure calculates the distance in frequency of occurrence between a "category profile" and a document. We use the measure to calculate the distance between the data from one domain, represented by a single document, and another domain, also represented by a single document.

We limited the four documents to just the first 1000 words each to make for direct comparison, since D2, at 1,315 words, is quite small. Given the unique words in such a small sample, we use a simple unigram model, splitting each document in half to test intra-document rank variation as well as rank variation between documents. We compare the rank of the 20 most frequently occurring words in each document against each of the other documents. This enables us to capture difference in rank only, since the top 20 unigrams are shared by all four documents.

Table 2 shows the rank comparison scores for each document. Lower scores indicate a higher relationship between two documents with respect to the rank order of their most frequently occurring words.

	D1	**D2**	**D3**	**D4**
D1	328.4	614.9	428.8	536.1
D2	753.4	587.8	1013.2	819.3
D3	568.8	837.3	432.1	568.5
D4	607.9	856.5	587.5	277.7

Table 2: Cross-domain frequency rank order

D4 is remarkable in two respects. First, it has a significantly lower intra-document variation, as shown on the diagonal in Table 2. Second, the 1 S.D. confidence interval for the inter-document rank order score does not overlap the intervals for the cross-document rank order scores, as shown in Table 3, where the top of the interval for the D4 intra-domain ranking is lower than the lowest score for each of the other domains when compared against D4.

Domain	Domain	score	SD	lowest score	highest score
D4	D4	277.7	80.9	196.8	358.6
D4	D1	536.1	132.5	403.5	668.6
D4	D2	819.3	133.4	685.9	952.7
D4	D3	568.5	155.1	413.4	723.6

Table 3: D4 intra-document score interval compared to D1, D2, and D3.

This lack of variation within D4 indicates that it is an outlier. We believe that these differences between D4 and the other domains suggested by this out-of-rank metric warrant caution in investing the time and cost involved in verifying the claims made by the narrator of D4.

The out-of-rank test separates D4 from the other domains as we had hoped since D4 represents the kind of data we want to avoid incorporating into a deception corpus. It contains only one critical lie: when asked if he has any idea where his wife is, the narrator answers only "No," with no additional verbal behavior that might indicate a lie. The narrator was subsequently found guilty of his wife's murder. His narrative describes his actions on the day of the murder, omitting all the details involving the murder.

4.2 New Domain Classification

To determine whether the distance metric would give us a means of successfully separating data that would be amenable to T/F classification from data that would not, we submitted a portion of all four domains to classifier testing. We used our own system for this test, although we believe the outlier status of D4 would be problematic for any system identifying deception because of the absence of lying in the narrative.

Each domain was annotated for the features in (1) and (2):

(1) Lack of commitment to a statement or declaration, where the speaker uses linguistic devices to avoid making a direct statement of fact. Five of the indicators fit into this class: (i) linguistic hedges including non-factive verbs and nominals, e.g. *maybe, I think, to the best of my knowledge*; (ii) qualified assertions, which leave open whether an act was performed, e.g. *I needed to get my inhaler*; (iii) unexplained lapses of time, e.g. *later that day*; (iv) overzealous expressions, e.g. *I swear to God*, and (v) rationalization of an action, e.g. *I was unfamiliar with the road*.

(2) Preference for negative expressions in word choice, syntactic structure and semantics. This class comprises three indicators: (i) negative forms, either complete words such as *never* or negative morphemes as in *inconceivable*;[i] (ii) negative emotions, e.g. *I was a nervous wreck*; (iii) memory loss, e.g. *I forget*.

Once we completed the feature annotation, we ran the annotated data through our system, which automatically discriminates between deceptive and truthful statements based on the density of features contained in each proposition in the data.
With the scores obtained from the system, we trained a Naïve Bayes classifier on within each domain, using 10-fold cross validation, as well as training using each domain and testing on each of the others. Table 4 shows within-domain accuracy rates, Table 5 cross-domain accuracy.

D1	68.2
D2	75.2
D3	59.0
D4	81.3

Table 4. Within domain accuracy (%) testing on features

The within-domain accuracy for D4 is startling until we consider that there were 32 verifiable claims, only one of which was false. Of more concern is the fact that the narrative effectively conceals a crime.

Train	Test	Accuracy
D1	D2	76.8
D1	D3	57.6
D1	D4	53.1
D2	D1	70.5
D2	D3	62.1
D2	D4	37.5
D3	D1	59.0
D3	D2	72.8
D3	D4	21.9
D4	D1	47.7
D4	D2	36.0
D4	D3	40.9

Table 5: Cross-domain classification results on features using a Naïve Bayes classifier (%)

While the review data (D3) is an outlier in the classification results, we attribute this, at least partially, to the system's dictionary, which was created for criminal data. The results for D4, on the other hand, are markedly below those of D3.

A NB classifier training and testing on unigrams (shown in Table 6), also shows the reviews as an outlier, as well as D4 as an extreme outlier.

However, the better results among the domains when features are used suggest that an attempt to incorporate the three domains into a corpus for verbal deception detection testing would be reasonable.

Train	Test	Accuracy
D1	D2	67.2
D1	D3	47.5
D1	D4	23.0
D2	D1	68,2
D2	D3	45.0
D2	D4	22.9
D3	D1	52.3
D3	D2	58.4
D3	D4	23.9
D4	D1	50.0
D4	D2	31.2
D4	D3	50.0

Table 6: Train/test classification results (%) on unigrams using a Naïve Bayes classifier.

5 Conclusion

In this paper we tested a simple distance metric, out-of-rank classification, to see if we could estimate the feasibility of building a T/F classification system for new a domain before the claims in the domain were verified. Through *n*-gram analysis on four domains with varying characteristics, we showed one of the domains, D4, to be an outlier with surprisingly little variation within the narrative. This result would have helped us avoid the expensive task of annotating D4 for ground truth only to discover that it had no verbally identifiable lies. While we currently do not have an explanation for the correlation between the absence of verbal deception in D4 and its outlier status, we plan to further analyze the differences between the language of D1-D3 and D4 for clues to the case of deception by omission, which D4 serves as a good model.

In addition, after training and testing interalia for D1-D3, we suggested that it would be reasonable to incorporate them as part of a single corpus. We hope the direction we have taken here to estimate the feasibility of including a new domain into a corpus with established ground truth will aid in the development of a common data set that would enable the development of a shared task in the computational detection of verbal deception.

Acknowledgements

We would like to thank Michael Schonwetter of Deception Discovery Technologies (DDTech) for development of the automatic tagging and scoring system used in this study, and the workshop reviewers for valuable suggestions and advice.

References

Joan Bachenko, Eileen Fitzpatrick and Michael Schonwetter. 2008. Verification and implementation of language-based deception indicators in civil and criminal narratives. In *Proceedings of the 22nd International Conference on Computational Linguistics-Volume 1* (pp. 41-48). CoLing.

William B. Cavnar and John M. Trenkle. 1994. N-gram-based text categorization. In *Proceedings of the Third Annual Symposium on Document Analysis and Information Retrieval*. pp.161-175.

David F. Larcker and Anastasia A. Zakolyukina. 2012. Detecting deceptive discussions in conference calls. *Journal of Accounting Research*, *50*(2), pp.495-540.

Song Feng, Ritwik Banerjee, and Yejin Choi. 2012. Syntactic stylometry for deception detection. In *Proceedings of the 50th Annual Meeting of the Association for Computational Linguistics: Short Papers-Volume 2* (pp. 171-175).

Vanessa W. Feng and Graeme Hirst. 2013. Detecting Deceptive Opinions with Profile Compatibility. *Proceedings of the Sixth International Joint Conference on Natural Langauge Processing.*

Tommaso Fornaciari and Massimo Poesio. 2011. Lexical vs. surface features in deceptive language analysis. In *Proceedings of the 13th International Conference on Artificial Intelligence and Law*, (pp. 2-8).

Tommaso Fornaciari and Massimo Poesio. 2014. Identifying fake Amazon reviews as learning from crowds. In *Proceedings of the 14th Conference of the European Chapter of the Association for Computational Linguistics*, (pp. 279-287).

Donato Hernandez Fusilier, Manuel Montes-y-Gómez, Paolo Rosso and Rafael Guzman Cabrera. 2015. Detecting positive and negative deceptive opinions using PU-learning. *Information Processing & Management*, 51(4), pp.433-443.

Rada Mihalcea and Carlo Strapparava. 2009. The lie detector: Explorations in the automatic recognition of deceptive language. In *Proceedings of the Association for Computational Linguistics – International Joint Conference on Natural Language Processing Conference Short Papers* (pp. 309-312).

Matthew L. Newman, James W. Pennebaker, Diane S. Berry, and Jane M. Richards. 2003. Lying words: Predicting deception from linguistic styles. *Personality and Social Psychology Bulletin*, *29*(5), pp.665-675.

Myle Ott, Yejin Choi, Claire Cardie, and Jeffrey T. Hancock. 2011. Finding deceptive opinion spam by any stretch of the imagination. *In Proceedings of the 49th Annual Meeting of the Association for Computational Linguistics: Human Language Technologies-Volume 1* (pp. 309-319).

Myle Ott, Claire Cardie, and Jeffrey T. Hancock. 2013. Negative Deceptive Opinion Spam. In *Proceedings of the 2013 Conference of the North American Chapter of the Association for Computational Linguistics: Human Language Technologies* (pp. 497-501).

Lina Zhou, Judee K. Burgoon, Jay F. Nunamaker, Jr. and Doug Twitchell. 2004. Automating linguistics-based cues for detecting deception in text-based asynchronous computer-mediated communications. Group Decision and Negotiation, 13(1), 81-106.

The Use of Second Life for Deception Detection Research

Stephen Kunath, Kevin McCabe
Center for the Study of Neuroeconomics
George Mason University
4400 University Drive, MSN 1B2
Fairfax. VA 22030, USA
skunath@gmu.edu, kmccabe@gmu.edu

Abstract

Detecting deception in natural language is a problem amenable to economic analysis. Economics typically assumes that individuals are self-interested, which leads them to perform actions in accord with their own goals. The field of experimental economics emerged to construct environments wherein human subjects make decisions so as to test economic hypotheses. Experimental economists recently have developed virtual worlds to better situate experiment subjects in more realistic environments. Virtual word experiments represent an exciting new area for deception research as they offer insight into individuals both acting out and communicating in accord with their intentions. This paper describes the use of virtual world experiments for economic research incorporating the detection of deceptive individuals.

1 Introduction

The fields of linguistics and economics typically assume different analytical techniques. Most peoples experience in an undergraduate economics class leaves them with the notion that the subject of economics contains only graphs. People then reasonably conclude that graphical depictions of supply and demand have little, if any, relation to speech acts. A result of the presumed limited applicability of economic modeling is that many do not realize that the graphs suggest how real life exchange actually operates. At the same time, as anyone should know, real life exchange requires some amount of communication between buyer and seller. Communication can take many forms from grunts and clicks, to the use of a human language, to an automated exchange of data between information systems. Fundamentally though human language will always play a necessary role in facilitating exchange between groups or individuals either directly or by helping different parties to negotiate the actual rules of exchange themself.

Suggesting that language and communication play some role in person to person exchange is correct but insufficiently descriptive. Language certainly plays a significant role in exchange as to effect a meeting of the minds between individuals there must be some common agreement concerning what is being exchanged and why. Potential obstacles can emerge during the communication phase of any round of negotiating exchange. An initial problem relates to the communicative sophistication of the parties involved in an exchange. One speaker could be a lawyer with an extensive background in negotiation while the other party might be a well educated layperson without specialized training. Differences between the individuals' verbal facility can lead to confusion or a wariness to engage in exchange for fear of manipulation. Another problem arises when two parties have different knowledge of things in the real world understood as an asymmetry of information between individuals. For example, a baseball card collector might know what a particular card is worth and believe the person he is trading with is unsure about the actual value and so the collector might offer a lower value than the market would suggest. Individuals possessing better information can then

Proceedings of NAACL-HLT 2016, pages 32–39,
San Diego, California, June 12-17, 2016. ©2016 Association for Computational Linguistics

reap an economic reward by using private information to their advantage.

The examples of problems found in exchange described above relate to communicative facility and information symmetry. When combined together one can reasonably expect an advantage to more well informed and verbally proficient exchange partners. Throughout history individuals have attempted to reduce the frequency of abuse in exchange by standardizing contract language and practices to reduce the advantages provided by enhanced verbal facility. To reduce information asymmetry consumer review services like CarFax collect and provide information to individuals about the actual history of a car, for example. Information asymmetry and superior communicative abilities, however, remain potential sources of discrepancies between individuals when the subject of exchange is an infrequently traded commodity. Unscrupulous parties can make use of the presence of asymmetries and verbal proficiency differences to deceive other people in an exchange.

2 Background

The ability to detect when other persons are being deceptive has always been a highly valued skill. Anecdotes abound in literature and personal histories of moments when one person grows suspect that another party was being deceptive. Detecting deception remains a perpetual challenge though, as it results from the fact that at any given time, one cannot immediately verify a claim that an another individual might make. Researchers have made progress in developing techniques to detect deception by studying what deception looks like. Identifying the characteristics of deceptive communication involves looking at numerous examples of dialogue and selecting those statements that contain deceptions. The modern study of deception has adopted a data driven approach which has resulted in many insights, but at the same time it has left open the question of how to obtain useful example data for research purposes. Different fields investigate deception using wholly different techniques aiming towards different goals. Some might be more interested in the contexts where deceptions can occur, while others might have more interest in the language differences between truthful and deceptive communications. One possible obstacle to progress in understanding and detecting deception could be the sheer number of different fields investigating the question such as psychology, computational linguistics, sociolinguistics, and economics. Each field uses its own data, methods, and models for the problem and a result has been less of an interdisciplinary approach than might otherwise be hoped for.

Much of the deception detection research investigates techniques for constructing datasets containing useful examples of deceptive communication. An obvious challenge constructing any deception dataset involves correctly labelling instances of deception and truth telling. Researchers have previously constructed datasets from online resources (Gokhman et al., 2012) as well as having human subjects intentionally engage in deceptive behavior (Almela et al., 2012). A necessary first step in the development of models of deceptive communication involves collecting and constructing appropriate corpora. It is crucial then that a deception corpus including instances of deceptive communication must also incorporate information concerning the actual behavior and goals of individuals as made manifest in their communication and also in their actions. That is, an ideal deception corpus would include both what a person said along with their motivation for saying it and whether what they said was true. Unfortunately, we cannot have complete knowledge of the current state of an individual's perspective on the world and as such we will never be capable of constructing an ideal corpus.

Absent an ideal corpus, insights from the field of economics present some interesting possibilities on the study of deception. For example, many people find it perfectly reasonable to assume that deception is a common part of many everyday transactions. Since economics assumes people are self-interested, one possible extreme assumption suggests people will be deceptive whenever they feel it serves their self-interest. Experience, however, suggests that people are not deceptive at all times. Anecdotal evidence instead suggests that individuals are more deceptive when the consequences of their deception are not severe or the probability of being caught is low. In point of fact, some economists have broken up deceptive behavior along the consequences that it might produce (Gneezy, 2005). The key distinction between different types of lies, as Gneezy suggests, involves understanding who might benefit from the deception. Deception then can be understood as benefiting or harming no one, the deceiver, the deceived, or some combination thereof. Here the economic conclusion of a possible economic outcome to the deceiver can then drive the communicative behavior to facilitate achieving the benefit. Seeing that there is an economic consequence to deception leads to the possibility that further research into deception could benefit by integrating insights from economics. Experimental economists have attempted to model institution formation in a number of different types of experiments that could be suggest a paradigm for further deception research (Kosfeld et al., 2009).

3 Experimental Environments

In recent years experimental economists have developed ever more sophisticated environments to test their models. One area that is particularly interesting for its potential with helping with research in deception involves the construction and use of virtual world experiments. One recent study constructed a virtual world to investigate the question of whether the discovery of natural resources can negatively impact a country (Al-Ubaydli et al., 2014). In their paper Al-Ubaydli et al. built an environment for their experiment subjects using Second Life. The factors the researchers varied were the presence of a resource in a particular country and how the subjects were able to communicate. While the economic question raised by the paper is interesting in its own right, the concern here is the part of the experiment that relates to controlling the subjects' ability to communicate. Al-Ubaydli et al. developed their model with a particular emphasis on controlling the ability of individuals to communicate based on the notion that communication is an essential component of institutional development and economic exchange.

Here it is worth considering that the term 'institution' carries a special meaning in economics. Generally it is meant to indicate the formal and informal rules of a society including property rights and dispute resolution (North, 1991). Economists suggest that for a society or group of individuals to succeed they must construct and maintain formal and informal institutions. If no one, for example, enforces property rights, then one would expect that people would alter their behavior to avoid issues arising from property questions like theft. Economists agree that good institutions are essential for economic flourishing, but then the next question is how to construct effective institutions.

A reasonable first guess is that good institutions involving humans do not appear randomly. Good institutions necessarily require trust between the different members of a society as manifested in cooperation and coordination. But trust, too, does not emerge spontaneously. Ostrom investigated the ingredients and steps for successful institutions to emerge. In Ostrom's view there must be both communication channels between individuals and some way to monitor compliance with rules (Ostrom, 2000). Communication is an essential aspect of monitoring since humans lack omniscience and cannot therefore know when someone is not living up to their side of an agreement. Unable to monitor all events, individuals must construct contracts whereby agreements are formed that require performances by each party and penalties for non-performance. In this agreement and performance component, the possibility remains that either party can deceive at any stage. That is, deception can occur when a party willingly agrees to something they never intend to do. Individuals can agree to perform their duties and then not do them, but they might realize that absent effective monitoring they can simply report that they completed their tasks. Deception can therefore occur during the negotiating involved in constructing an agreement or it can happen after an agreement takes place where an individual deceives as to what they have done.

The ability to verify that an individual is telling the truth constrains the deceptive behavior of individuals especially in the presence of negative consequences for deceiving. In the real world it is difficult for individuals to monitor everything related to a particular agreement, but virtual worlds offer the opportunity to monitor the actions of individuals and compare them to whatever claims they make in their communication. With this in mind, some of the tools from experimental economics seem particularly well suited to the problem of deception research as experimental economists can construct environments and incentives for subjects to deceive to enhance their own benefits. Virtual world experiments can be used for experiments that also allow rich communication between players with the added benefit of being able to monitor all player actions. Thereby the data produced by virtual world experiments provide both the actual messages communicated by individuals and also the insight into what actions an individual actually took. Appropriately constructed virtual world experiments then can offer researchers an incredible new tool to peer into deceptive behaviors and their manifestation in communication.

4 Example Experiment

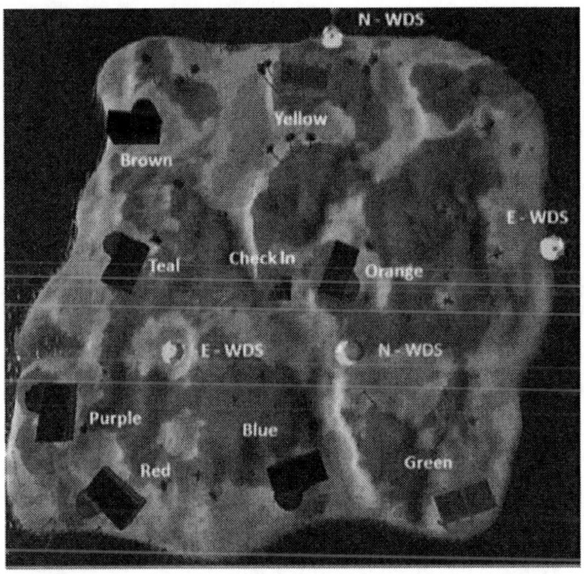

Figure 1: An overhead image of the Second Life Island

Coordinating activities between a group of people is always difficult but can be especially challenging when people have different incentives. This problem is further compounded when individuals are not capable of precisely monitoring the activity of their collaborators. To that end we have begun constructing virtual world experiments that focus on collective action problems with the hope of getting useful data on how people use communication to coordinate towards socially optimal solutions. Our interest concerns experimental designs where the incentives for the group and individual subjects are in conflict. Creating experiments where subjects must make choices between fulfilling their own incentives or supporting the outcome of the group allows for the possibility of deceptive behavior. Our experiments are instrumented so we can record what a subject communicates and also all of their actions.

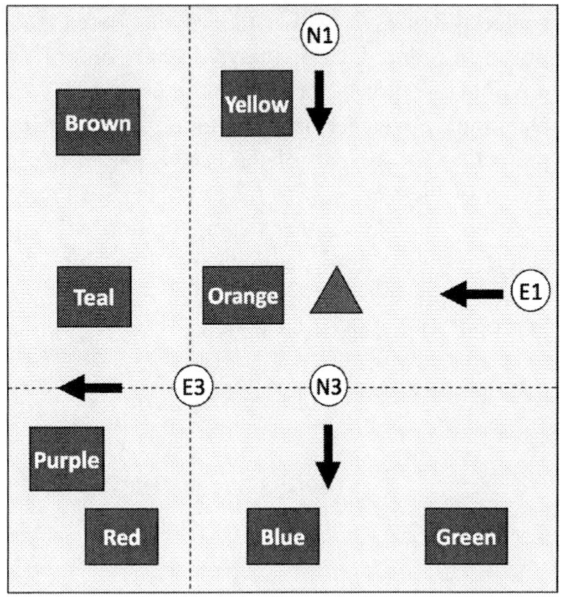

Figure 2: A depiction of the subjects' houses, squares, and weather defense stations, circles. Storms come from either the north or east edge. The arrows depict the areas of the island that would be protected by operating a weather defense station in the presence of a storm coming from the appropriate direction.

Our lab conducted one experiment where eight subjects are placed together on an island inside of a virtual world constructed in Second Life. We refer to the experiment as "Hurricane Island." Each subject is assigned a color and is referred to by that color throughout the experiment. The island contains eight separate houses and each subject is assigned to a particular house. Figure 1 provides an overhead view of the island. The experiment subjects earn money while they stay in their homes. In our experiment the subjects could earn 40 cents per minute while they were inside their homes. However, for the subjects to earn the full amount their house must not become damaged. If a house does become 50% damaged, for example, the subject could only earn up to 20 cents a minute. The island is subject to external events similar to natural disasters, in this case hurricanes, that can damage houses with some frequency throughout an experiment session. Hurricanes appeared on the island approximately every five minutes. Subjects could defend either their house individually or portions of the island by operating what was called a weather defense station. Figure 2 shows the locations of the subjects' houses as well as the weather defense stations. In Figure 2 storms travel in only one of two possible directions, North to South, or East to West. Operating a weather defense station only provides protection for the part of the island behind the location of the station. So, for example, in Figure 2 operating the N3 weather defense station will only be effective for storms coming from the North and will only prevent damage from occurring to the Purple, Red, Blue, and Green houses.

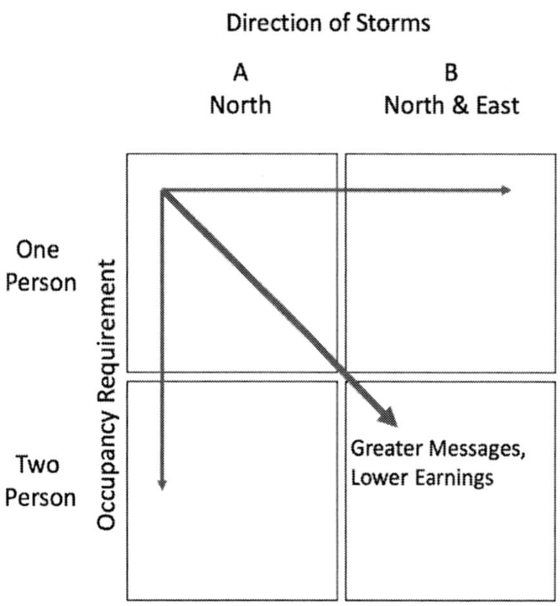

Figure 3: A depiction of the 4 treatment types. The occupancy requirement axis refers to the number of subjects that must occupy a weather defense station to make it operational. The horizontal axis represents whether storms come just from the North or come from both the North and East.

Since subjects are being paid to occupy their houses, doing any other activity such as defending their house individually, repairing their house after it is damaged, or operating a weather defense station represents a loss in earnings. Obviously, each subject could simply decide to defend their own home, but this would mean that the group would not be capable of maximizing the groups total income. The maximum social outcome can only occur when subjects coordinate and have individuals protect the entire island from the effects of the hurricanes by going to the appropriate weather defense stations placed on the island. Our research goal was to investigate institution formation and so we constructed 4 separate treatments for the experiment. We ran a total of 16 sessions across the four treatments and each session lasted approximately 90 minutes. The different treatments involved altering the number of originating directions of the storms and the occupancy requirements for the weather defense stations. Figure 3 provides a graphical overview of the different treatments. In Figure 3, coordination becomes more complex when moving treatments in the diagonal direction towards the lower right cell. The basic treatment, as seen in the top left cell of Figure 3, involved all storms coming from the same direction, North, and requiring only one person in a weather defense station to make it operational. More complex treatments involved having storms that could originate from one of two different directions and also requiring that two subjects be inside a weather defense station to make it operational. Moving from only one person being necessary to operate a weather defense station to two persons places a heavier burden on coordination as now at least two people will not be generating income in their houses and they must also agree on what weather defense station to meet at. Storms originating from two different directions also increases the burden of coordinating as it would require having the appropriate number of people in two separate weather defense stations until the subjects determine the direction of the storm.

An additional design concern related to the placement of the weather defense stations on the island. Each defense station protected the parts of the island behind the station itself. Four weather defense stations were placed in different positions such that one would have some defense stations that would only protect a limited part of the island. It is important to note that the weather defense stations were different distances from each subject's house. Any time they spent defending their house, the island, repairing their home, or traveling to a weather defense station entailed that they were not producing anything and thereby their possible payout would be reduced. Since some weather defense stations were closer to some houses it remained possible that some individuals or groups could decide to only protect their area of the island. The fact that distances were different for each subject and those distances affected their payout could dispose players to form groups to protect only limited parts of the island or it could dispose a player to simply defend their own home.

Throughout the experiment subjects were able to communicate with each other with the chat system provided by Second Life. For the subjects to achieve the optimal social outcome some amount of planning and cooperation is necessary between all the subjects involved in the experiment. When the players in our experiment use the chat system every subject is able to read the message so there is no private communication. One ideal solution solution to achieve the social maximum would entail that subjects find some way of rotating the responsibility of operating the weather defense stations throughout the experiment session. Analyzing the chat data in the earlier parts of the experiment sessions we noticed that subjects frequently attempt to cooperate by identifying a rotation for operating weather defense stations. There is no way, however, for each subject to effectively monitor the behavior of other subjects at all times. and this provides subjects with the possibility of not fulfilling their responsibility. This allows individuals to deceive others by agreeing to do something they have no intention of doing or simply stating that they did something that others cannot verify. In the context of this experiment the subjects could only really determine that another subject had not fulfilled their part of a coordination program by experiencing damage to their houses. At the same time, since the experiment is in a virtual world we configured appropriate monitoring to record the activities of subjects and then compared those actions to whatever messages had been communicated. Comparing the log of subject messages to the actions subjects actually performed allowed us to identify different types of non-cooperative behavior including deception.

Speaker	Message
Yellow	where was teal and orange
Yellow	im getting damaged
Teal	i hv covered
Purple	me too
Red	im getting damaged?
Yellow	teal and orange you did not do it right
Purple	wher s orange?
Yellow	teal and orange were both supposed to go to n1
Yellow	everyone needs to read there messages
Teal	i am at n1
Teal	but no one came
Yellow	orange fault
Teal	orange are you there
Teal	we all loose
Teal	coz of you
Red	earth to orange lol
Yellow	orange hasnt sent a message the whole time
Orange	hey, look at ur manuals again and do the math
Orange	you stand a chance of making a lot more by staying home and defending

Table 1: Example of session communications

Due to the nature of the experiment and the amount of time, groups of subjects used the early minutes of the session to organize their operation of the weather defense stations. A common strategy

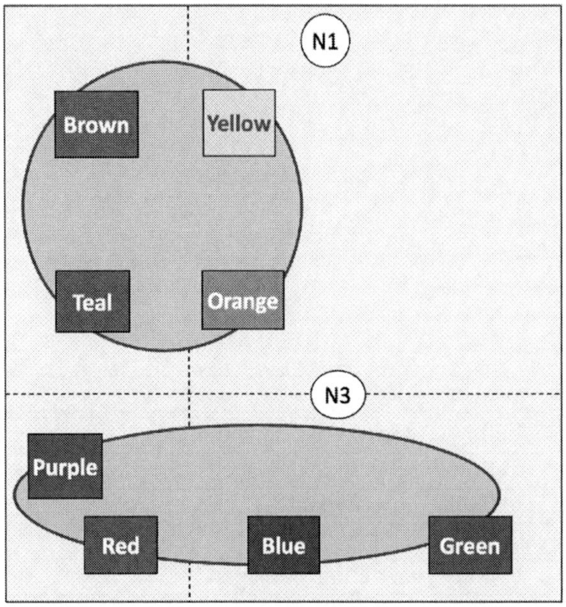

Figure 4: Game theory predictions for storms originating from the north. The players in the top part of the map have an incentive to defend at the N1 weather defense station and thereby protect the whole island. Players in the lower part of the map have an incentive to operate the N3 weather defense station and only protect their part of the island.

that was employed was to have subjects rotate who would take turns operating the weather defense stations. While the strategy was simple, it still meant that enforcement was a challenge as individual subjects could not verify that someone was operating the weather defense station until it was too late. Table 1 provides an example of communication from an experimental session. In the experiment session where the chat took place two subjects are required to operate the weather defense station but only one person has shown up. The orange player has not fulfilled their obligation to operate the weather defense station and is not being communicative with the other subjects for an extended period of time. Eventually the orange player suggests that the reason for their absence is due to a belief that they can have a larger payout if they simply defend their homes individually which is, in fact, incorrect. Since the experiment was designed with different distances to weather defense stations it is reasonable to assume that some subjects would determine that only defending a part of the island is in their best interest.

If one analyzes the layout of the experiment using game theory, it becomes clear that different groups of subjects have different incentives to defend only parts of the island. Figure 4 shows the game theory predictions for storms originating from the North. The specific prediction for North originating storms is that group in the upper half of the map has an incentive to operate the N1 weather defense station. When the subjects in the upper part of the map operate the N1 defense station they are both protecting themselves and also creating a public good for the players in the lower part of the map. One would then predict that players in the lower portion of the map would only be interested in operating the N3 weather defense station which would leave the players in the upper part of the map without any defense. As the treatments become more complex with two subjects required to operate a weather defense station and two possible storm directions the benefits derived from non-cooperative play increase. Creating incentives to not cooperate thereby indirectly encourages the possibility of deceptive communication as subjects would be interested in having other people provide weather defense for the island while they free ride on the benefit.

5 Conclusion

This paper has provided an example showing how the tools and techniques of experimental economics can be used to construct situations where individuals have an incentive to engage in deceptive communication with other subjects. Collecting both the communication data and the actual actions of the individual subjects a virtual world experimental paradigm can create new corpora for research into deception in natural language. In order to assist further research in this area we would like to release several example experiments and tools we used to construct and operate this experiment to the community so that researchers can formulate and construct their own experiments useful for research into deceptive behavior. Our belief is that by leveraging economic theory and techniques developed in experimental economics researchers can construct different experimental scenarios where subjects have incentives that induce behaviors in individuals and create situations where deception should occur. At the same time, by making use of virtual world technology researchers can be effectively omniscient and compare the communication of individuals to their actions in the experiment. To help others interested in constructing a virtual world experiment we have begun to produce documentation and examples. The documentation for this effort along with working code will be available at `http://gmucsn.github.io/VirtualWorldExperimentTutorial`

References

[Al-Ubaydli et al.2014] Omar Al-Ubaydli, Kevin McCabe, and Peter Twieg. 2014. Can More Be Less? An Experimental Test of the Resource Curse. *Journal of Experimental Political Science*, 1(01):39–58, March.

[Almela et al.2012] Ángela Almela, Rafael Valencia-Garc 'i a, and Pascual Cantos. 2012. Proceedings of the Workshop on Computational Approaches to Deception Detection. pages 15–22. Association for Computational Linguistics.

[Gneezy2005] Uri Gneezy. 2005. Deception: The Role of Consequences. *The American Economic Review*, 95(1):384–394.

[Gokhman et al.2012] Stephanie Gokhman, Jeff Hancock, Poornima Prabhu, Myle Ott, and Claire Cardie. 2012. Proceedings of the Workshop on Computational Approaches to Deception Detection. pages 23–30. Association for Computational Linguistics.

[Kosfeld et al.2009] Michael Kosfeld, Akira Okada, and Arno Riedl. 2009. Institution Formation in Public Goods Games. *The American Economic Review*, 99(4):1335–1355.

[North1991] Douglass C North. 1991. Institutions. *The Journal of Economic Perspectives*, 5(1):97–112.

[Ostrom2000] Elinor Ostrom. 2000. Collective Action and the Evolution of Social Norms. *The Journal of Economic Perspectives*, 14(3):137–158.

Identifying Individual Differences in Gender, Ethnicity, and Personality from Dialogue for Deception Detection

Sarah Ita Levitan & Yocheved Levitan
Columbia University

Guozhen An
CUNY Graduate Center

Michelle Levine
Columbia University

Rivka Levitan
Brooklyn College CUNY

Andrew Rosenberg
Queens College CUNY

Julia Hirschberg
Columbia University

Abstract

When automatically detecting deception, it is important to model individual differences across speakers. We explore the automatic identification of individual traits such as gender, native language, and personality, using acoustic-prosodic and lexical features from an initial non-deceptive dialogue. We also explore predicting success at deception and at deception detection, using the same features.

1 Introduction

Automatic deception detection is a critical area of research for a variety of disciplines, from computational linguistics and psychology to law enforcement, military, and intelligence agencies. One of the challenges in this work is the variation across individuals and cultures in deceptive behavior. In previous work on deception in American English speech, (Hirschberg et al., 2005) developed automatic deception detection procedures trained on spoken cues. These procedures have accuracies 20% better than human judges. While identifying common characteristics of deceivers, they also noticed many individual differences in deceptive behavior, e.g., some subjects raised their pitch when lying, while some lowered it; some tended to laugh when deceiving, while others laughed more while telling the truth. They also discovered that human judges' accuracy in judging deception could be predicted from their scores on the NEO-FFI Personality Inventory (Costa and MacCrae, 1992), suggesting that such simple personality tests might also provide useful information in predicting individual differences in deceptive behavior itself (Enos et al., 2006).

Differences in verbal deceptive behavior in across cultures have been identified by several researchers (Feldman, 1979; Cody et al., 1989), who have found that culture-specific deception cues do exist. (Fornaciari et al., 2013) found that personality information can be successfully used as features for deception detection. In our previous work (Levitan et al., 2015a), we conducted a study of cross-cultural deceptive speech, using a large scale corpus of Mandarin Chinese (MC) and Standard American English (SAE) native speakers. We found that including gender, native language, and personality scores in addition to acoustic-prosodic features improved classification performance.

Such work is promising, but requires ground-truth knowledge of these individual traits. For example, it requires NEO-FFI personality scores, which may be impractical to collect in a real-world deception situation. In this work, we address this problem. Specifically, we aim to answer the following question: How much information can be automatically learned from a short dialogue with a subject? We use a portion of the corpus described in (Levitan et al., 2015b) for this study. This part is an initial dialogue between an experimenter and each subject, a 3-4 minute truthful conversation in which the subject answers simple, open-ended questions. Using this subset, we extract acoustic-prosodic and lexical features, and train classifiers to identify gender, native language (American English or Chinese), and personality. We are also interested in whether we can automatically predict from a short dialogue if a subject will be better or worse than average at detec-

Proceedings of NAACL-HLT 2016, pages 40–44,
San Diego, California, June 12-17, 2016. ©2016 Association for Computational Linguistics

tion deception and at lying. All of this information can be useful for downstream deception detection.

In Section 2, we describe the corpus collection and the methods used for transcription and segmentation of the data. Section 3 describes the features used in classification experiments, and Section 4 presents the results of our classification experiments for gender, native language, personality, success at deception, and success at deception detection. We conclude in Section 5 and discuss future research.

2 Corpus

The Columbia deception corpus (Levitan et al., 2015b) consists of within-subject deceptive and non-deceptive speech from native speakers of SAE and MC, both speaking English. (Native language is defined as spoken at home until age 5.) It includes data from 172 subject pairs — 122.5 hours of speech. To our knowledge, this is by far the largest corpus of cleanly recorded deceptive and non-deceptive speech collected and transcribed, with self-identified truth/lie labels. We employed a fake resume paradigm in which pairs of subjects were recorded playing a lying game, alternating between interviewing their partner and being interviewed about answers to a set of 24 biographical questions. As interviewees, they are instructed to convince their interviewer that everything they say is true. As interviewers, they are told to try to identify when the interviewee is lying and when they are telling the truth. To motivate them, their compensation depends on their ability to deceive while being interviewed, and to judge truth and lie correctly while interviewing. As interviewer, they receive $1 each time they correctly identify an interviewees answer as either lie or truth and lose $1 for each incorrect judgment. As interviewee, they earn $1 each time their lie is judged to be true, and lose $1 each time their lie is correctly judged to be a lie by the interviewer.

We collected demographic data from each subject and administered a NEO-FFI (5 factor) personality test (Costa and MacCrae, 1992), assessing: *Neuroticism, Extraversion, Openness to Experience, Agreeableness Conscientiousness.*

We also collected a 3-4 minute baseline sample of speech from each subject for use in speaker normalization, in which the experimenter asks the subject open-ended questions (e.g., What do you like best/worst about living in NYC?). Subjects are instructed to be truthful in answering. Once both subjects have completed all the questionnaires and we have collected both baselines, they begin the lying game.

Transcripts for the recordings were obtained using Amazon Mechanical Turk (https://www.mturk) (AMT). Three transcripts for each audio segment from different 'Turkers' were obtained, and combined using rover techniques (Fiscus, 1997), producing a rover output score measuring the agreement between the initial three transcripts. For clips with a score lower than 70%, transcripts were manually corrected; we needed to hand correct 9.7% of clips.

Speech was segmented into InterPausalUnits (IPUs) – speech from a single speaker separated by 50ms or more (Hirschberg et al., 2005) – using Praat (Boersma and Weenink, 2002). The silence detection was done using intensity thresholding with Praat. We observed IPU segmentation errors resulting from this method, in which areas of speech were identified as silence and had humans hand-correct the IPU segmentation. The experiments in this paper use the 238 baseline files that have been corrected to date. This consists of 25,424 IPUs, in total about 16 hours of speech.

3 Features

We extracted two feature sets for our machine learning experiments: acoustic-prosodic and lexical. Acoustic-prosodic features are extracted from IPUs. We used Praat to extract the following acoustic-prosodic features from each IPU: f0 min, max, mean, median, stdv, mean absolute slope; intensity min, max, mean, stdv; jitter, shimmer. The first six features are different measures of the fundamental frequency, the physical correlate of pitch. The next four are measures of a correlate of perceived loudness. The last two features are measures of voice quality, variation in vocal fold behavior which leads to listeners' perception of the harshness or creakiness or breathiness of the voice. We also estimated speaking rate by calculating the ratio of voiced to total frames and included this as a feature. All these features have been proposed in the literature on deception as possible indicators of deception (DePaulo et al., 2003). Once we extracted these features at the IPU level, we aggregated them into a feature vector for each speaker by averaging the features across the speaker's IPUs. We did this for all features except for minf0 and maxf0, where we used the min of all minf0 and max of maxf0 as aggregated features.

We used Linguistic Inquiry and Word Count (LIWC) (Pennebaker et al., 2001) to extract the lexical features. LIWC is a text analysis program that analyzes text by computing word counts for 72 linguistic dimensions. LIWC dimensions have been used in many studies to predict outcomes including personality (Pennebaker and King, 1999), deception (Newman et al., 2003), and health (Pennebaker et al., 1997). We performed minor pre-processing of the transcripts before running LIWC, as recommended by the manual (e.g. removing spaces from phrases, such as "Idon'tknow").

4 Classification Experiments

Using these features, we experimented with different machine learning models and feature sets to predict the following information about the speakers: gender, native language, personality, success at deception, and success at deception detection. Gender and native language ground truth were collected via demographic forms, and personality scores were obtained from the NEO-FFI. Success at deception is measured by the percentage of lies that the subject tells which are judged as true by the interviewer. Success at deception detection is measured by the percentage of correct judgments that the subject makes as interviewer. To conduct our experiments, we needed to convert the numeric values for personality scores, lies, and judgments into nominal values. For NEO-FFI scores, we used the population norms for personality detailed in (Locke, 2015) to divide subjects into high, average, and low for each of the five personality factors, for male and for female subjects separately. For success at deception and detection, we binned subjects into high and low, using the mean as a cutoff point. For each classification task, we compared the performance of four machine learning algorithms, all using the scikit-learn implementation (Pedregosa et al., 2011): SVM, logistic regression, AdaBoost, Random Forest. All evaluation was done using 10-fold cross validation.

4.1 Gender and Language Identification

We found that the Random Forest classifier performed best for gender and language identification for all three feature sets; therefore only those results are reported here. Table1 displays the gender classification results, measured by accuracy, precision, recall, and f-score. The majority class baseline is 61% for gender (female), and 57% for ethnic origin (SAE). Intuitively, the acoustic-prosodic features are highly predictive of gender. It is interesting that LIWC categories are also somewhat predictive of gender, with an f-score of .76 – despite the fact that all subjects answered almost the same questions. Some of the most useful categories were 'home', 'anxious', and 'negative emotion', which all were predictive of 'female'. On the other hand, 'anger', 'certainty', and 'money' categories were predictive of male. Note that combining LIWC features with acoustic-prosodic features very slightly improves over using acoustic-prosodic features alone. On the other hand, as shown in Table 2,

Table 1: Gender classification results

Features	acc	prec	rec	f-score
Prosodic	.94	.94	.96	.95
LIWC	.70	.69	.86	.76
Combined	.94	.94	.98	.96

LIWC features are more predictive than acoustic-prosodic features for native language/ethnicity identification. Combining both feature sets results in the best performance, with an f-score of .78. When analyzing the LIWC categories, we find that the punctuation counts are especially useful for this task. For example, use of 'apostrophe' is predictive of English, while dash is predictive of Mandarin. In our transcription, dashes are used to represent false starts, so it makes sense that this is a marker of less fluent speech. Apostrophes were used exclusively for transcribing contractions, which are less commonly used by non-native speakers of English, so it is plausible that apostrophes are predictive on English.

It is important to note that our subjects are all answering the same questions in their baseline sam-

Table 2: Language classification results

Features	acc	prec	rec	f-score
Prosodic	.65	.64	.40	.49
LIWC	.84	.82	.7	.76
Combined	.81	.88	.68	.78

ples of speech. Therefore, it is quite impressive that LIWC features can predict both gender and language with .76 f-score by capturing the variation in how the questions were answered. We find that gender can be predicted with 94% accuracy and language with 84% accuracy using simple features from 3-4 minutes of conversational speech.

4.2 Personality Identification

We repeated the same experiments for personality detection, this time with a 3-class classification problem (low, med, high) for each of the 5 factors. Table 3 shows the results for AdaBoost and Random Forest, which were the two best performing classifiers for personality. As expected, the three classes are highly unbalanced, with the majority of subjects falling into the average class, and a small percentage in the high and low classes. Because of this, we focus our analysis on comparing the f-scores of the different classifiers and feature sets, in order to obtain a more meaningful comparison of the performance of the classifiers over the max-frequency baseline. As seen in Table 3, the best performing model for each factor is significantly better than the baseline. The baseline classifier always predicts the majority class for each of the five factors, and table shows the f-score of this baseline classifier. The relative improvements in f-score range from 38% (Extroversion) to 64% (Openness to experience), and the absolute improvements in f-score range from 10% to 22%. When we rank the LIWC features that contribute the most to the models, we find interesting results. For N-score, 'power' and 'money' dimensions are the most useful; for E-score, 'drives' and 'focusfuture'. For O-score, 'interrogation' and 'focus past' are useful; for A-score, 'social' and 'assent'; and for C-score, 'work' and 'time' are highest. Most of these are intuitive and show the power of using LIWC features for personality detection. Although these results show significant improvements

Table 3: Personality classification results, f-scores

Features	Model	N	E	O	A	C
Prosodic	AB	**.43**	.30	.48	.46	.35
	RF	.39	.33	.45	.40	.33
LIWC	AB	.38	.34	.45	.41	**.42**
	RF	.38	**.36**	**.56**	**.47**	.32
Combined	AB	**.43**	.33	.48	.40	.34
	RF	.41	**.36**	.53	**.47**	.39
Baseline	–	.28	.26	.34	.32	.27

over the baseline, there is much more to investigate in predicting personality traits. A possible reason for the low performance is that self-reported personality scores might not correlate with personality perceptions of others (including machine learning models). Additionally, we use classes based on population distributions that might not be the best fit for our data. For example, the scores are based on participants of all ages, while our subjects are mostly college students. Our approach might benefit from using personality scores from a student population if these were available.

4.3 Deception and Deception Detection

We repeated the experiments to predict success at lying and at detecting lies simply from the norming data, in which people were presumably telling the truth. The baseline is 53% for success at deceiving, and 52% for success at detecting deception. For deception detection, our best classifier (AdaBoost, prosodic+LIWC) achieved an accuracy of 61%. When we included binned NEO-scores, gender and language as features in addition to the prosodic and LIWC feature sets, we achieved an accuracy of 65%, a 25% relative increase over the majority class baseline and a 13% absolute increase. We find that none of models using any feature sets were able to beat the baseline accuracy for predicting success at lying. Despite previous findings that success at deception is correlated with success at deception detection (Levitan et al., 2015b), our classifiers were only able to predict success at judgments. When we examine the ranked features for deception detection, the most useful features include speaking rate and LIWC categories'focus present', and 'bio'. Perhaps people who are present-focused are more conscientious and therefore better judges of others' behavior. This is supported by our previous findings that conscientiousness is somewhat correlated with success at deception detect deception.

5 Conclusions and Future Work

In this work we have identified acoustic-prosodic and lexical features which can predict gender, native language/ethnicity, and personality using only a short non-deceptive dialogue. We experimented with using all these features to predict success at deception detection and at deception itself, with significant results only for deception detection. In future work we will experiment with different methods of binning personality scores and different ways of modeling deception detection and deception success. We will also evaluate if our prediction of personality, gender, and ethnic background can help in predicting truth and lie in our larger corpus as effectively as ground truth.

Acknowledgments

This work was partially funded by AFOSR FA9550-11-1-0120 and by NSF DGE-11-44155.

References

Paul Boersma and David Weenink. 2002. Praat, a system for doing phonetics by computer. *Glot international*, 5(9/10):341–345.

Michael J Cody, Wen-Shu Lee, and Edward Yi Chao. 1989. Telling lies: Correlates of deception among chinese. *Recent advances in social psychology: An international perspective*, pages 359–368.

Paul T Costa and Robert R MacCrae. 1992. *Revised NEO personality inventory (NEO PI-R) and NEO five-factor inventory (NEO FFI): Professional manual*. Psychological Assessment Resources.

Bella M DePaulo, James J Lindsay, Brian E Malone, Laura Muhlenbruck, Kelly Charlton, and Harris Cooper. 2003. Cues to deception. *Psychological bulletin*, 129(1):74.

Frank Enos, Stefan Benus, Robin L Cautin, Martin Graciarena, Julia Hirschberg, and Elizabeth Shriberg. 2006. Personality factors in human deception detection: comparing human to machine performance. In *INTERSPEECH*.

Robert S Feldman. 1979. Nonverbal disclosure of deception in urban koreans. *Journal of Cross-Cultural Psychology*, 10(1):73–83.

Jonathan G Fiscus. 1997. A post-processing system to yield reduced word error rates: Recognizer output voting error reduction (rover). In *Automatic Speech Recognition and Understanding, 1997. Proceedings., 1997 IEEE Workshop on*, pages 347–354. IEEE.

Tommaso Fornaciari, Fabio Celli, and Massimo Poesio. 2013. The effect of personality type on deceptive communication style. In *Intelligence and Security Informatics Conference (EISIC), 2013 European*, pages 1–6. IEEE.

Julia Bell Hirschberg, Stefan Benus, Jason M Brenier, Frank Enos, Sarah Friedman, Sarah Gilman, Cynthia Girand, Martin Graciarena, Andreas Kathol, Laura Michaelis, et al. 2005. Distinguishing deceptive from non-deceptive speech. In *EUROSPEECH*.

Sarah I Levitan, Guzhen An, Mandi Wang, Gideon Mendels, Julia Hirschberg, Michelle Levine, and Andrew Rosenberg. 2015a. Cross-cultural production and detection of deception from speech. In *Proceedings of the 2015 ACM on Workshop on Multimodal Deception Detection*, pages 1–8. ACM.

Sarah Ita Levitan, Michelle Levine, Julia Hirschberg, Nishmar Cestero, Guozhen An, and Andrew Rosenberg. 2015b. Individual differences in deception and deception detection. In *Proceedings of Cognitive 2015*. Cognitive.

Kenneth Locke. 2015. NEO scoring. `http://www.webpages.uidaho.edu/klocke/neo_scoring.htm`. 2016-03-07.

Matthew L Newman, James W Pennebaker, Diane S Berry, and Jane M Richards. 2003. Lying words: Predicting deception from linguistic styles. *Personality and social psychology bulletin*, 29(5):665–675.

Fabian Pedregosa, Gaël Varoquaux, Alexandre Gramfort, Vincent Michel, Bertrand Thirion, Olivier Grisel, Mathieu Blondel, Peter Prettenhofer, Ron Weiss, Vincent Dubourg, et al. 2011. Scikit-learn: Machine learning in python. *The Journal of Machine Learning Research*, 12:2825–2830.

James W Pennebaker and Laura A King. 1999. Linguistic styles: language use as an individual difference. *Journal of personality and social psychology*, 77(6):1296.

James W Pennebaker, Tracy J Mayne, and Martha E Francis. 1997. Linguistic predictors of adaptive bereavement. *Journal of personality and social psychology*, 72(4):863.

James W Pennebaker, Martha E Francis, and Roger J Booth. 2001. Linguistic inquiry and word count: Liwc 2001. *Mahway: Lawrence Erlbaum Associates*, 71:2001.

Individual Differences in Strategic Deception

Scott Appling and **Erica Briscoe**
Georgia Tech Research Institute
Georgia Institute of Technology
Atlanta, GA, United States
scott.appling@gtri.gatech.edu
erica.briscoe@gtri.gatech.edu

Abstract

While text-based deception in computer mediated communication has been studied, e.g., Zhou (2005) and Duran et al. (2010), there has been less focus on the differentiation of strategies for deception, especially those which may manifest in modern communication, such as found in social media. In this paper, we extend our previous work on the evaluation of linguistic indicators to strategic deception (Appling et al., 2015), by evaluating the relationship between personality and deceptive strategy use and the utilization of linguistic features for inferring both (personality and deception). We find that even with a relatively small corpus, there is evidence that personality is related to particular deception strategies, though in short social media communications, these personality traits are difficult to infer using standard linguistic measures (e.g., LIWC). We also describe the corpus we collected from an experiment in which subjects engaged in deception through a social media platform.

1 Introduction

The ubiquitous nature of social media has significantly magnified the communicative ability of individuals and groups and changed the way many individuals receive information (Lenhart et al., 2010). Consequently, this increased access has enlarged the influence opportunity space, where deception is a commonly utilized influence method (Buller et al., 1994). A theme of our research is focused on the evaluation of how findings from previously studied communication methods, e.g., Burgoon et al. (1996), differ as a result of both changing communication styles and the affordances provided by modern communication platforms (i.e., social media).

Research into "tells" that indicate when a person is lying have been a subject of interest for many years, e.g. (Ekman and Friesen, 1969), and has resulted in a substantial list of potential cues (DePaulo et al., 2003). These cues to deception are usually described as those that occur significantly more or less frequently when a communicator expresses an untruth as compared to the truth. These indicators may differ according to the point of view of the receiver and sender (Anderson et al., 1999) and have been identified in widespread communications, such as the 2016 United States election coverage (Scott, 2016). While our previous work evaluated the detection of deceptive statements and deception strategies using linguistic cues (Briscoe et al., 2014; Appling et al., 2015), here we describe our evaluation of how individual differences, specifically as represented through different personalities, may affect strategic deception and be inferred from an experimentally collected corpus.

2 Eliciting Deception Strategies

Past work has characterized multiple deception strategies (Rubin, 2010; Turner et al., 1975; Burgoon et al., 1996), roughly organized into the four main types described below.

- **Falsification** - e.g. lies, contradictions, or "distortions"
- **Exaggeration** - e.g. more or modified information via superlatives

Proceedings of NAACL-HLT 2016, pages 45–52,
San Diego, California, June 12-17, 2016. ©2016 Association for Computational Linguistics

- **Omission** - e.g. secrets (missing information), half-truths (less or modified information), or 'concealment"

- **Misleading** - e.g. topic changes, irrelevant information, equivocation, or 'diversionary responses"

To evaluate the use of the previously described set of strategies, we conducted human subject experimentation to simulate an online social network environment where participants were tasked with engaging in a conversation involving a decision making task where they were encouraged to employ deception. We also administered a personality inventory to assess each participant's standing on the dimensions contained within the Five Factor Model (FFM) of personality (McCrae and Costa Jr, 1999): openness, conscientiousness, extroversion, agreeableness, neuroticism. Then we extracted lingustic features that were found to be statistically significant predictors of related personality traits. We then report on an analysis on the use of linguistic features for predicting deception strategies based on individual-trait level psychological constructs (personality).

The rest of the paper is organized as follows. First we describe the experimental setup and the collected data. Next, we discuss the deception strategies corpus that was created. We then discuss the results of two analyses: one related to predicting deception strategy on personality trait scores and a second on using psycholinguistic features to predict personality. We conclude with a discussion of the implications of the results and future directions

3 Deception Experiment

To study deception strategies in social media, we designed and ran an in-lab experiment where individuals were asked to use a social media platform for a group decision making task. The task allowed us to control the scenario as well as topics of discussion within the conversations.

Seventy-five subjects recruited from the student body at Georgia Tech participated in the experiment. Each subject was seated at a computer station and asked to use a mock online social media site (FaceFriend, see Figure 1). The mock site was intended

Figure 1: Example screenshot of the *FaceFriend* web-based interface used in the experiment. The interface was designed to mimic commonly used social media platforms.

to resemble a popular social networking site. Participants completed three pre-experiment surveys, including a personality test and a survey regarding their social media and email usage, so as to ensure consistency among familiarity with social media. The procedure and results reported below are from one of a three part experiment, the other two parts of which are not reported here (as they centered on the perception of deception and credibility, see Briscoe et al. (2014) and Briscoe et al. (2013) for details of the other parts of the study. Subjects were paid for their participation.

Participants were asked to read a scenario involving a group decision making task called the "subarctic survival problem" (Eady and Lafferty, 1969). Participants were instructed to log in to a mock social media platform, *FaceFriend*, and to communicate with another individual to decide the best ranking of items to take from a crashed plane site in an Arctic environment. Participants were further instructed to advocate for a specific ranked list of items, also provided, and to do so using deception, when possible. To ameliorate differences in creative ability, subjects were provided with expert explanations for the advantages provided by each item; these could be used as the basis for creating deceptive statements. For example, the list of items included an Axe, which the expert noted could be used to chop wood. Lastly, participants were ostensibly informed that the other conversation participant would be unaware of any potential deception. The participant's conversational partner was a confederate member of the research team, sitting in another room. During the conversation, to minimize variation in the confederate's response language, the confederates communicated using a list of statements conceived beforehand as suitable decision making conversation responses (e.g., "What about the canvas?"). After discussing the items for 12 minutes, the interaction was concluded, and subjects were asked to log out of FaceFriend.

After the end of the conversation, participants were shown the list of statements they made during the task in a browser windows and asked to identify which ones were deceptive using a check box. Upon indicating a particular statement was deceptive, participants were prompted to categorize their strategy for that particular message. The possible strategies to select were the same types described in Section 2. Multiple strategies were allowed to be designated. An additional category, "Other", was available that allowed free response space for any strategies that the subject felt did not fit into one of the four provided categories. Table 3 displays example deceptive statements, as identified by subjects, in each category.

4 Deception Corpus

The deception corpus contains all statements made by participants during the deception experiment described earlier. These include truthful and deceptive statements. For each statement we provide a boolean indicator as to whether or not the participant annotated that statement as enacting one or more of the deception strategies described in Section 2. [1]

Table 4 lists the frequencies of each identified strategy in the corpus as indicated by the subjects. Statements which subjects identified as containing multiple strategies are not included. On average, the misleading strategy was the most likely strategy to be employed by participants and the omission strategy the least likely. Table 1 lists summary statistics about the statements in the corpus. Sentiment and subjectivity scores were calculated for each statement, using the method described by De Smedt and Daelemans (2012). Table 2 provides the descriptive statistics of the distribution of personality variables across our subject pool, as well as relevant demographic information.

5 Analysis

5.1 Linguistic Cues and Deception Strategies

After excluding statements falling below a minimum one word threshold[2], 393 statements (including truthful statements) were used in a one-way multivariate analysis of variance to determine the effect of deception strategy on linguistic cue levels. The 8 linguistics cues studied are listed in Table 1. A statistically significant difference was found between the different deception strategies and truthful statements on the combined linguistic cues dependent variables $F(32, 1406.654) = 1.93, p < 0.001$; Wilks' $\Lambda = 0.852$; partial $\eta^2 = 0.039$, though no specific differences were found between specific strategies. Follow-up univariate ANOVAs showed a statistically significant difference between the use of deception strategies and no strategy using a Bonferroni adjusted α level of 0.025. Tukey post-hoc tests showed: there were less average verb cues for truthful statements compared to exaggerations ($p < 0.001$) and compared to misleading statements ($p < 0.019$) ($M = 4.695; SD = 0.274; M = 6.657; SD = 0.419; M = 6.222, SD = 0.413$, respectively); lower mean word count for truthful statements compared to exaggeration statements ($p < 0.019$;M=20.024; SD=0.899; M=25.086; SD=1.376, respectively); and lower mean Fleish-Kincaid score cues for truthful statements compared to exaggeration statements ($p < 0.005$; $M = 3.228; SD = 0.438; M = 5.993; SD = 0.670$, respectively).

[1] The collected corpus is available by emailing the authors.

[2] Exclusion of one-word statements was based on the fact that these statements were almost exclusively one-word responses (i.e., "yes" or "no") to questions posed by the confederate. While these responses may exhibit untruths, the authors feel that the reflection of deception is mostly based in the content of the interrogation, rather than the response itself.

Table 1: Deception Conversation Corpus Summary Statistics per Subject

Variable	Mean	Std. Dev.	Min.	Max.
Per Subject				
Statement Count	6.00	3.62	1.00	17.0
Strategy: Exaggeration	1.20	1.07	0	4.00
Strategy: Misleading	1.31	1.21	0	6.00
Strategy: Omission	0.80	1.01	0	5.00
Strategy: Falsification	1.03	1.37	0	8.00
Per Comment				
Avg. Modifiers	2.85	1.09	0.75	6.00
Avg. Pausality	2.38	1.02	0	4.66
Avg. Verbs	5.68	2.19	2.00	12.33
Avg. Words	23.43	7.33	8.00	41.00
Avg. Word Length	3.82	0.27	3.10	4.79
Avg. Fleish-Kincaid Score	4.91	3.40	-3.62	12.20
Avg. Sentiment	0.17	0.12	-0.17	0.41
Avg. Subjectivity	0.40	0.12	0.17	0.75

Note: Sentiment scores range between -1 (extremely negative) and 1 (extremely positive); Subjectivity scores range between 0 (completely objective) and 1 (completely subjective).

Table 2: Participant Demographic and Personality Statistics

Variable	Mean	Stdev.	Min.	Max.
Age	22.5	4.8	18	45
Openness	25.1	4.8	15	35
Conscientiousness	35.9	6.4	18	49
Extroversion	29.8	6.2	17	42
Agreeableness	28.7	3.0	21	35
Neuroticism	19.6	6.3	8	34
Gender	**Female**	35	**Male**	40

5.2 Predicting Deception Strategies using Personality

Hierarchical multiple regression analyses were conducted using each deception strategy as the dependent variable with each FFM personality trait as a predictor including gender as a blocking variable. See Table 5 for details on each regression model. From the analysis, we find that only *extroversion* was a predictive trait, found to influence the *omission* deception strategy during deceptive communications, $R^2 = .139, F(2,72) = 5.823, p < .01$. The direction of the relationship suggests that less extroverted individuals are more likely to use an omission strategy.

5.3 Predicting Personality using Psycholinguistic Lexical Features

Given that there was a relationship found between *extroversion* and the *omission* strategy, we are then motivated leverage other work centered on automatically deriving personality from text, in order to derive indicators for extra version. To create our indicators, we utilize previously identified psycholinguistic features from (Mairesse et al., 2007) related to predicting extroversion from text. A hierarchical multiple regression analysis was conducted using the *omission* deception strategy as the dependent variable with the following LIWC features (found to be indicative of extroversion by Mairesse (2007): 1st Person Plural, 1st Person Singular, Articles, Body, Family, Filler, Inclusion, Negations, Positive Emotion, Social Processes, Tentativeness, Total Pronouns.

The ANOVA omnibus F-test proved insignificant, $F(13,74) = 0.840, p = 0.617$, indicating no statistically significant relationships existed between the LIWC features for predicting omission; no follow-up analyses were conducted.

Table 3: Examples of Deception Strategies

Identified Deception Strategy	Participant's Statement During Experiment	Participant's Explanation
Exaggeration	"the axe is awesome, and should be the first priority. In that cold weather we'll need definitely need something to chop firewood with"	"in this statement, I'm playing along with a positively framed question. I agree with the other guy and exaggerate how awesome the axe is, and how it should definitely be the first priority"
Misleading	"well I think the canvas should be number 4, it could be used for shelter protect us from the harsh winds, but should be below the Crisco because that could be used to store water and be a signal "	"This was misleading because the canvas would probably be more important than the crisco because the canvas could hlave been used as a blanket that produced warmth and the crisco would not be as useful because you could just eat snow"
Falsification	"I think the axe, newspaper, crisco, cavas, wool, and pistol should be brought in that order. I itemized them from most importance to least. we can disgard lower priority items if the trip gets rough"	"I was trying to get list across without really taking time to actually reason through why I am choosing that order."
Omission	"I agree that the wool should be ranked 5th, but the crisco is much more useful than the canvas because it can be used for fire which is essential."	"I didn't compare the cost/benefit of the two items, only what I liked about the crisco"

Table 4: Frequency of Deception Strategies

	Exaggeration	Misleading	Omission	Falsification
Count	67	69	41	45

6 Discussion

The goal of the work was to evaluate how personality (as a means of characterizing individuals) can be used to predict the types of deception strategies that those individuals might use in short, social media-based conversations. The secondary goal was to determine if, given a limited social media corpus, those personality characteristics found related to strategic deception could be derived based on linguistic features. While we did find a relationship between personality and deception strategies, where less extroverted individuals are more likely to use an *omission* strategy, we did not find evidence that the *extroversion* trait can be accurately derived from this same text using only the extroversion indicators identified by Mairesse et al. (2007). The difficulty in inferring traits from content-derived psycholinguistic features has been identified in other investigations (Adali and Golbeck, 2012; Schwartz et al., 2013); however, the use of additional features, both linguistic, e.g. (Appling et al., 2013)) and non-, e.g. (Adali and Golbeck, 2012), can improve trait prediction.

Additionally, we determined that several linguistic features (e.g., the number of verbs in a statement) are significantly different across truthful and deceptive statements, but only for certain types of deception strategies. In previous work we evaluated the use of discriminative models for classifying decep-

Table 5: Hierarchical Multiple Regression Predicting Strategy from Gender and Personality

	Omission Strategy				Misleading Strategy			
	Model 1		Model 2		Model 1		Model 2	
Variable	**B**	β	**B**	β	**B**	β	**B**	β
Constant	0.820**		1.982**		1.295**		-0.642	
Gender	0.295*	0.292	0.352*	0.349	-0.180	-0.150	-0.232	-0.193
Openness			0.160	0.034			0.006	0.024
Conscientiousness			0.060	0.009			0.020	0.108
Extroversion			-0.039*	-0.239			0.024	0.123
Agreeableness			-0.046	-0.137			-0.002	-0.005
Neuroticism			-0.024	-0.151			-0.021	0.108
R^2	0.085		0.139		0.023		0.055	
F	6.807*		5.823*		1.680		0.666	
	Exaggeration Strategy				**Falsification Strategy**			
	Model 1		**Model 2**		**Model 1**		**Model 2**	
Variable	**B**	β	**B**	β	**B**	β	**B**	β
Constant	1.189**		-1.926		1.021**		2.708	
Gender	-0.161	-0.152	-0.167	-0.158	-0.079	-0.058	-0.067	-0.049
Openness			-0.001	-0.004			0.031	0.110
Conscientiousness			-0.002	-0.011			0.032	0.154
Extroversion			-0.004	-0.021			-0.010	-0.043
Agreeableness			0.106	0.297			-0.107	-0.236
Neuroticism			0.014	0.084			-0.014	-0.063
R^2	0.010		0.100		0.003		0.066	
F	1.715		1.263		0.245		0.802	

Note: * $p < .05$, ** $p < .001$

tion strategies (Appling et al., 2015) based solely on linguistic features. There, we found that some features were more discriminative for some strategies. For example, the most predictive feature for discriminating falsification was in the LIWC negation category (e.g., using 'no', 'not', 'never'), which we found unsurprising given that these statements are often disagreements in response to the statements made by the other participant. Those features, however, were not found to be significantly associated with any particular strategy in the current study. Also, in that study, the *omission* strategy was the most difficult to discriminate, using a train random forest classifier (Breiman, 2001). This result was not surprising given that, by definition, the omission of information does not provide linguistic content from which to derive features. Interestingly, and perhaps unfortunately, it is this same strategy that we find most related to personality dimensions, i.e., extroversion, in the current study.

An obvious question from this and related studies focuses on the appropriate amount of text that is needed to infer individual-level traits, such as these inferences are as accurate as direct measurement. In Golbeck et al. (2011) the authors conducted analysis with 176 participants who averaged 42.6 words from combined social media status updates, whereas Mairesse et al. (2007) captured on average 766.4 words per subject. Other works, e.g. Nie et al. (2014), give no indication concerning the amount of text being used per individual. These questions are especially relevant given that social media communications are likely highly variable, exhibiting fluctuations arising from a variety of factors, such as mood (Bradley and Mogg, 1994).

7 Future Work and Conclusion

Given the likely influence of modern communication platforms on human communication styles, utilizing linguistic-based indicators for deception is a difficult and evolving challenge. One, likely fruitful, method of addressing this challenge is to leverage work that has been done on characterizing individuals as a means of using that characterization for predictive tasks; however, given the brevity and informality of social media communications, much more work must be done to create methods for utilizing this kind of text. Related to the use of lexical psycholinguistic features, we see opportunity with recent work in vectorized word representations to develop semantic features based on lexical qualities that weight observations smoothly. Future work will continue to evaluate the efficacy of using informal text-based characterizations as means of predicting communication strategies.

Acknowledgments

This material is based upon work supported in part by the Defense Advanced Research Projects Agency (DARPA) under Contract No. W911NF-12-1-0043.

References

Sibel Adali and Jennifer Golbeck. 2012. Predicting personality with social behavior. In *Proceedings of the 2012 International Conference on Advances in Social Networks Analysis and Mining (ASONAM 2012)*, pages 302–309. IEEE Computer Society.

D Eric Anderson, Bella M DePaulo, Matthew E Ansfield, Jennifer J Tickle, and Emily Green. 1999. Beliefs about cues to deception: Mindless stereotypes or untapped wisdom? *Journal of Nonverbal Behavior*, 23(1):67–89.

D Scott Appling, Erica J Briscoe, Heather Hayes, and Rudolph L Mappus. 2013. Towards automated personality identification using speech acts. In *Seventh International AAAI Conference on Weblogs and Social Media*.

Darren Scott Appling, Erica J Briscoe, and Clayton J Hutto. 2015. Discriminative models for predicting deception strategies. In *Proceedings of the 24th International Conference on World Wide Web Companion*, pages 947–952. International World Wide Web Conferences Steering Committee.

Brendan P Bradley and Karin Mogg. 1994. Mood and personality in recall of positive and negative information. *Behaviour research and therapy*, 32(1):137–141.

Leo Breiman. 2001. Random forests. *Machine learning*, 45(1):5–32.

Erica J Briscoe, D Scott Appling, Rudolph L Mappus IV, and Heather Hayes. 2013. Determining credibility from social network structure. In *Proceedings of the 2013 IEEE/ACM International Conference on Advances in Social Networks Analysis and Mining*, pages 1418–1424. ACM.

Erica J Briscoe, D Scott Appling, and Heather Hayes. 2014. Cues to deception in social media communications. In *System Sciences (HICSS), 2014 47th Hawaii International Conference on*, pages 1435–1443. IEEE.

David B Buller, Judee K Burgoon, JA Daly, and JM Wiemann. 1994. Deception: Strategic and nonstrategic communication. *Strategic interpersonal communication*, pages 191–223.

Judee K Burgoon, David B Buller, Laura K Guerrero, Walid A Afifi, and Clyde M Feldman. 1996. Interpersonal deception: Xii. information management dimensions underlying deceptive and truthful messages. *Communications Monographs*, 63(1):50–69.

Tom De Smedt and Walter Daelemans. 2012. Pattern for python. *The Journal of Machine Learning Research*, 13(1):2063–2067.

Bella M DePaulo, James J Lindsay, Brian E Malone, Laura Muhlenbruck, Kelly Charlton, and Harris Cooper. 2003. Cues to deception. *Psychological bulletin*, 129(1):74.

Nicholas D Duran, Charles Hall, Philip M McCarthy, and Danielle S McNamara. 2010. The linguistic correlates of conversational deception: Comparing natural language processing technologies. *Applied Psycholinguistics*, 31(03):439–462.

Patrick M Eady and James Clayton Lafferty. 1969. *The subarctic survival situation*. Experimental Learning Methods.

Paul Ekman and Wallace V Friesen. 1969. Nonverbal leakage and clues to deception. Technical report.

Jennifer Golbeck, Cristina Robles, and Karen Turner. 2011. Predicting personality with social media. In *CHI '11 Extended Abstracts on Human Factors in Computing Systems*, CHI EA '11, pages 253–262, New York, NY, USA. ACM.

Amanda Lenhart, Kristen Purcell, Aaron Smith, and Kathryn Zickuhr. 2010. Social media & mobile internet use among teens and young adults. millennials. *Pew Internet & American Life Project*.

François Mairesse, Marilyn A Walker, Matthias R Mehl, and Roger K Moore. 2007. Using linguistic cues for the automatic recognition of personality in conversation and text. *Journal of artificial intelligence research*, pages 457–500.

Robert R McCrae and Paul T Costa Jr. 1999. A five-factor theory of personality. *Handbook of personality: Theory and research*, 2:139–153.

Dong Nie, Zengda Guan, Bibo Hao, Shuotian Bai, and Tingshao Zhu. 2014. Predicting personality on social media with semi-supervised learning. In *Proceedings of the 2014 IEEE/WIC/ACM Conference on Web Intelligence and Intelligent Agent Technologies*, pages 158–165, Washington, DC, USA. IEEE Computer Society.

Victoria L Rubin. 2010. On deception and deception detection: Content analysis of computer-mediated stated beliefs. *Proceedings of the American Society for Information Science and Technology*, 47(1):1–10.

H Andrew Schwartz, Johannes C Eichstaedt, Margaret L Kern, Lukasz Dziurzynski, Stephanie M Ramones, Megha Agrawal, Achal Shah, Michal Kosinski, David Stillwell, Martin EP Seligman, et al. 2013. Personality, gender, and age in the language of social media: The open-vocabulary approach. *PloS one*, 8(9):e73791.

Leslie Scott. 2016. Across new jersey, bands of local islamophobes crusade to drive islam underground, Mar.

Ronny E Turner, Charles Edgley, and Glen Olmstead. 1975. Information control in conversations: Honesty is not always the best policy. *Kansas Journal of Sociology*.

Lina Zhou. 2005. An empirical investigation of deception behavior in instant messaging. *Professional Communication, IEEE Transactions on*, 48(2):147–160.

Association for Computational Linguistics
209 N. Eighth Street
Stroudsburg, Pennsylvania 18360

ISBN 978-1-5108-2522-2

9 781510 825222

CURRAN ASSOCIATES INC.
proceedings.com